Jump!

10 simple rules
to guarantee success
in your career

Buchi Onwugbonu

Jump!

First published in 2016 by

Panoma Press Ltd,
48 St Vincent Drive, St Albans, Herts, AL1 5SJ, UK,
info@panomapress.com
www.panomapress.com

Book layout by Neil Coe.

Printed on acid-free paper from managed forests.

ISBN 978-1-784521-02-8

The right of Buchi Onwugbonu to be identified as the author of this work has been asserted in accordance with sections 77 and 78 of the Copyright, Designs, and Patents Act 1988.

A CIP catalogue record for this book is available from the British Library.

This book is available online and in bookstores.

Contents

Introduction 4

**10 rules to follow to guarantee success
in your career** 13

Chapter 1 It's your career 15

Chapter 2 Be very clear on why you got hired 29

Chapter 3 Respect the performance management
process – don't fight it! 37

Chapter 4 There are others that matter,
besides your line manager 47

Chapter 5 Do more than your role requires…
and then some 59

Chapter 6 Seize opportunities to reinvent yourself 69

Chapter 7 Don't do it alone 79

Chapter 8 Become an excellent communicator..............95

Chapter 9 Master the art of networking.....................109

Chapter 10 Execute like a true professional..................119

Conclusion 135

About the Author..145

Introduction

I was at a leadership conference a few years ago, one of those sessions that have a mixture of external speakers and speakers from within the company. It was a three-day training event, very intense, and it was day number two when this external speaker walked on to the stage. I will try my best to recount his story as it is something that has remained with me ever since.

He walked on to the stage and looked up at about 500 of us, in the theatre-style room, and said:

"10 guys who had never done professional diving before decided to attempt, for the first time, a three-metre springboard dive…"

Then he stopped talking. He walked from the centre of the stage to one end then back again to the centre, all the time looking at the audience. Then he continued: "Just to check how many people were paying attention, how many people took the three-metre dive?" he asked.

Some people immediately called out "10" – a response that made him smile as he watched the same people, myself included, reconsider their answers. Slowly the significance of the question dawned on us.

Ten people *decided* to jump but how many *actually* jumped? The true number is unknown unless you were at the scene to actually see how many went ahead and jumped, but the reality here is the majority wouldn't. Why? Because in life, deciding to do something, whether it's taking a three-metre springboard dive or learning a new language is one thing, actually doing it is another.

You see, it isn't the guys who just read about diving, watch movies and take classroom lectures on diving that go on to become great divers. It's the guys who climb up to that springboard and jump. Fair enough, the first time they do, they will most likely score a 1 out of 10 or even a zero because they will get everything wrong, but eventually, if they apply a combination of theoretical and practical learning consistently, they will, most likely, one day become great at diving. But they have to take that first jump.

In this book, you will read about very useful tips that, if applied, could have a profound effect on your career. Some of the suggestions will be uncomfortable so will take you out of your comfort zone. You will find that it will be easier to agree with the action but justify why what you're currently doing will suffice. If you find yourself thinking this, stop, and realise that if you keep doing what you've always done you will keep getting the same results.

To make real progress in anything in life requires you to be willing to do more things out of your comfort zone. More than you've been doing up until now, so if you're serious about really moving your career forward you need to commit to taking action. Be prepared to jump!

Recognising that this won't be easy for most people, I thought it would be useful to walk through three common traits that will help. You will find these traits in most successful people you know and if you don't score yourself at least a six out of 10 on each of them you need to start working on developing them as soon as possible.

The first one is **Self-Discipline.** I'm sure you all know what this means but let me offer a simple definition that is worth reflecting on, every time you find yourself flagging a bit:

Self-discipline is doing what you need to do, when you need to do it, whether you like it or not.

So simple, so true, but very often disregarded.

The next time you find yourself struggling with taking an action you know you're supposed to take, please remember this simple statement and just go ahead and do what you know you need to do. We will revisit this subject later in the book.

The second one is **Resilience**. Again, this isn't going to be an unfamiliar term for you but worth calling out. Knowing you need to do something and having the self-discipline to do it isn't sufficient if you don't have a strong resilience to overcome the challenges life will throw at you on a daily basis. Self-discipline will get you out of bed and on to the pavement for a run you planned the night before but you will need a strong resilience to keep running when your legs start to feel like jelly and your mind tells you you're too tired to continue.

There are tons of books and articles on how to build up your resilience, so if you are struggling in this area I suggest you do something about it. Some of the proven ways to improve your resilience include a good diet and regular exercise; being involved in a charitable cause; taking time out regularly to spend with friends and family and also on your hobbies outside of work.

The final one is **a strong WHY**. Having a strong reason for doing something is probably the biggest single factor that can make the difference between success and failure. It is this bigger reason or larger purpose that would motivate you to be more disciplined and get up at 5 a.m. after a busy night before. It is also this reason that will keep you working up until midnight when you feel your resilience failing. Conversely, this determination strengthens your resilience and will make it easier the next time you find yourself in a similar situation.

Why I wrote this book

I have been working as a professional now for about 15 years. I started my career in finance, later moved into consulting then most recently I have been running a global service organisation. During this time I have been fortunate to have worked with very senior and influential mentors. I have watched these guys closely and from a distance and learned and adapted techniques that have made a material difference in my career to date. Consequently, over the last five years I have also actively coached and mentored aspiring leaders both within and outside my organisation.

During the last five years, from experience of my own challenges and challenges presented by some of my mentees, I started to collate a list of some of the most common problems people face when trying to take their career from one level to the next. For example, moving from senior manager to a GM or Director role or moving into their first executive role or, even more common, moving from team member to their first leadership role.

Some of the other challenges have been understanding how to navigate a complex corporate organisation with multiple geographic and functional units. Or moving from a back office function like HR or finance into a customer-facing role in operations or sales. The list goes on…

What I have attempted to do in this book is provide a set of rules that, if followed, will enable you to navigate these challenges successfully and move your career to the next level and beyond.

How this book is structured

I have organised this book into 10 rules, each of which covers a particular career topic and addresses a number of challenges that you may be facing at work.

Chapter 1 – It's your career begins with the fundamental principle that you are in charge of your career, nobody else. It talks about starting first with deciding what you want, understanding where you are, reviewing your options and identifying your next steps, then taking action immediately.

Chapter 2 – Be very clear on why you got hired takes you to the very starting point of every employment. Now I can imagine you might say: "But I've already been in my job for a year so this won't be relevant for me". I disagree.

I encourage you to read this chapter. At worst, it would be a confirmation of some good practice you already have in place and, if so, well done. Please keep this up. Or, at best, you will come across some very useful tips that you can implement immediately and begin to see a difference in how you are perceived by your team.

Chapter 3 – Respect the performance management process – don't fight it! goes on to explore how to ensure you make the performance management process work for you rather than against you.

Chapter 4 – There are others that matter, besides your line manager introduces your wider stakeholder community, their importance and how to get them on your side to help build your career successfully.

Chapter 5 – Do more than your role requires… and then some talks about one of the most effective ways of getting promoted.

Chapter 6 – Seize opportunities to reinvent yourself talks about exploiting opportunities to make a strong first impression when you start a new role. It also talks about how you can take advantage of a negative performance review to reinvent yourself and establish a new reputation as a strong performer.

Chapter 7 – Don't do it alone talks about the benefits of working with coaches, mentors and career sponsors and how to find them. You don't need to do it alone. No very successful person has, so why should you?

Chapter 8 – Become an excellent communicator talks about how to improve your communication skills to make sure your message gets across as intended, with particular emphasis on the most common form of written communication in business today: emails.

Chapter 9 – Master the art of networking introduces the subject of networking, why you should do it and tips on how to build and maintain a network that will help move your career forward.

Finally, **Chapter 10 – Execute like a true professional** talks about what you need to do to bring all the other rules into action and be able to guarantee success in your career.

While each chapter can stand on its own as a complete article with learning points on a particular area, I urge you to read the book in sequence because each chapter also builds on from the previous one and culminates with the specific focus on execution in Chapter 10.

Making sure this book works for you

To make sure this book works for you, I urge you not to read through it like a novel. When you find something useful, stop and consider how it can be applied. Most smartphones now have a note-taking facility so use it to take notes on what you can apply that day. Be very specific and, even better, create a calendar entry for what you will do and describe it in detail. This way you are making a commitment to yourself.

Complete each of the exercises included in the book before continuing to the next section. It will be easy to say I'll just read on and will come back later, but the likelihood of you coming back to complete it is very low. You will be much better off completing the exercises in sequence.

What will make the difference is the action you take, not the knowledge you gain. A man who can read but doesn't is no different from a man who cannot read. Read, apply, read, apply, read, apply... hopefully you get the message. Stay in active mode throughout the book. Inevitably some of the actions you take will be uncomfortable to begin with. Not doing it or ceasing to finish what you started will be the easier option. I encourage you to continue. Continue until it becomes a habit then it will become difficult to stop.

10

rules to follow to guarantee success in your career

1 It's your career

2 Be very clear on why you got hired

3 Respect the performance management process – don't fight it!

4 There are others that matter, besides your line manager

5 Do more than your role requires... and then some

6 Seize opportunities to reinvent yourself

7 Don't do it alone

8 Become an excellent communicator

9 Master the art of networking

10 Execute like a true professional

#1
It's your career

Where you are in your career today is a sum total of your thoughts, choices and actions to date. Now since your actions are determined by your thoughts and the choices you make, it stands to reason that you are totally responsible for where you are right now. And it begins with your thoughts, starting with a visualisation of what path you wish to follow in your career. Just like a designer starts with a mental picture which eventually gets brought to life, as chief architect of your career, a good place to begin is thinking about what it is you would like to achieve during your career journey.

It's your career so where would you like it to take you? You may already be on the right track and want to take it to the next level. On the other hand, it may be time for you to consider a change: a change in company, in career or maybe a change in location. The choice is entirely yours. This is YOUR career.

Begin with the end in mind

It is important before you continue to take some time to think about where you would like your career to go. At this point I urge you to avoid thinking about where you are today as this will most likely limit your ambition. This is normal. For example, if you have spent the last five years in finance and been promoted twice, it is understandable that in thinking about the next five years you would expect a similar trajectory. It will also be difficult to consider a role in a few years' time as head of digital marketing as the path from where you are today just wouldn't seem feasible. I encourage you to abandon this line of thought, at least for now. The time will come when we have to consider where we are and blah, blah, blah… for now, put that to one side and concentrate on where you would like to be.

Exercise 1

Take a blank sheet of paper and a pen and find somewhere to sit where you won't be disturbed for at least half an hour. Now write down what your future career would look like. Imagine if you had the power to make anything possible, what would you do for work?

One way I find useful is to put yourself into a social environment. Imagine five years from now that you were in a restaurant having lunch with a close colleague and someone that they know came up to them to say hello. After the brief pleasantries they turn to you enquiringly. How would you like your colleague to introduce you? Try completing this sentence:

"… and this is John. John and I work together. John is responsible for…"

Or you can use other variations like:

"John runs the…", "John is the…" or "John is the expert at…"

Pay attention to the first thoughts that come into your mind when you attempt to complete the sentence. Write them down so you don't forget. Try to also extend the conversation further. For example:

"And this is John. John runs the chemicals division of GE. A 20,000 people organisation spread out across the Americas region. John is the expert when it comes to launching new products in the market…"

What you're doing here is letting your inner desires come to the surface in a totally unrestricted environment. Try to write down whatever comes to mind as much as possible. After the exercise, go through your list and take note of the things you read that get you excited. Try to make this a fun exercise. You have nothing to lose. You can also try doing it with a close friend who you trust and read back to each other what you each wrote down and discuss what it means.

If this approach isn't for you then try the more serious route. List down the top three careers you would like if you had no constraints. Your present career can be one of these but doesn't have to be. Now write down for each career the specific job title. Go through all three, if you came up with three, and select one as your target role for the next five years.

Congratulations. You have just done what only less than 10% of the working population does. Some people might struggle to come up with more than one aspirational role; others may have more than five and struggle to select one. If you find yourself in this position, just remind yourself that this is just a fun exercise. At least for now anyway. It is more important that you try it out and make a decision than to agonise over what you select for weeks, months or even years as some people do. The exercise shouldn't take more than 30 minutes and this is definitely enough time to come up with a good starting point. You don't have to hit the mark the first time but you will at least get some direction.

If you read up to this point without doing the above exercise, I strongly suggest you pause and find time to do it before continuing with the rest of the book. You can leave the house 30 minutes earlier on your way to work and find a café somewhere to have a coffee while you do the exercise. It is important that you get into the action habit from now on so avoid skipping this part and moving straight to the next section. Once you've got some clarity on what you want to do, you will be ready to review your current situation.

Back to reality

Imagine inputting a destination into your satellite navigation system but the system had no way of identifying your current position. How likely is it to give you a route? Impossible, right? So now you have an idea of what excites you, the next step is to understand exactly where you are today. This is time for some deep reflection so some quiet time is definitely required. I would suggest you find about 45 minutes at a time that you won't be interrupted. First thing in the morning, if you're a morning person, or late at night when everyone else has gone to bed. Or you can block out time during the day to go to a coffee shop if you're okay working with noise in the background, or whatever works for you. Key thing is to avoid any interruptions so you can immerse yourself in the exercise.

Exercise 2

Using a blank sheet of paper for capture, walk through each of the following sections and state where you are today.

Experience, qualifications and training: In this section, try to list out your current level of experience, e.g. finance manager or finance director. Your exposure

and breadth of experience, e.g. P&L experience of
£200m cost base, across Europe. List any particular
language skills, etc. An up-to-date CV should suffice
for this section.

Strengths and weaknesses: This section will
require more thinking. Reflect on your career to date
and in particular the last two years. What are your key
strengths? One way to identify your key strengths is to
imagine you are in a room filled with people. What is
it that you are better at than most of the people in that
room with you? Those are your key strengths. Can
you give examples of how you have demonstrated that
strength in the past month? What are your weaknesses?
What are the things you are worst at compared to most
people? How well have you applied your strengths?
Have you consciously pursued roles that exploit your
strengths more fully? How have you approached your
weaknesses? Have you sought any help to address them
or have you avoided jobs that require these skills more?

Natural tendencies: Examine your natural
tendencies as you think through how you got to where
you are today. What decisions did you make about
your career during the past two years? Are you where
you had planned to be? Did you consciously choose to
go after your existing job or did you settle for it while
you waited for something else? Look at the last two
roles before your current role and ask yourself the
same questions. Do you see a pattern in your career
path to date?

These three areas are not exhaustive but are sufficient to get you to understand thoroughly not just where you are but why and how you got there. The changes you will need to make will become clearer as you look forward to where you aspire to be. If you spotted any good habits, great. Take note of them as you will need to continue with these. If you spotted any bad habits, great. Take note of them as you will need to come up with a plan to break them.

Once you have completed the above exercise, it will be time to continue to the next section.

Weigh up your options

You have identified where you would like to go and now have a thorough understanding of where you are in relation to this aspiration. The next step is to consider your options and I encourage you to broaden your criteria as much as you can without losing focus. This way you increase your chances of success tremendously. There are three main areas most people consider. No single one is better than the other as they are all largely dependent on where you are and where you would like to go. It will also be dependent on how much effort you are willing to put in and for how long, to get the desired result.

Let us consider each in turn.

Staying with your existing employer and moving up the chain: In most cases, remaining in your existing organisation to move up the chain within the current function should be the easiest to pursue. It can also be the most difficult if you haven't built a solid enough reputation during the time that you have been there.

Staying with your existing employer but moving to a different function: Moving to a different function can be tricky but not impossible. The extent to which you can do this would be dependent on a number of factors including how well you can identify and sell your transferable skills and the strength of your network (more on this later).

Moving to another company and remaining in the same function or to change function: While moving to another company can be difficult, it is sometimes inevitable. Switching functions at the same time will be extremely difficult but not impossible. This would depend on how marketable you are and the external contacts you have and their ability to connect you with opportunities out there.

There is an old tale, *The Acres of Diamond*, a story about a man who sold his home to use the money to fund his trip to faraway lands in search of diamonds since he had been hearing stories of so many who had found diamonds and become rich beyond their wildest dreams. After years of frustration and bitter disappointment, one day he committed suicide. Meanwhile, the man who had purchased his house was playing in the yard and one day found an interesting stone in the garden. He picked it up, cleaned it and placed it on his mantelshelf at home. One day a visitor spotted it and after taking a closer look, asked him where he got it from. The owner of the land, puzzled, asked why and the visitor informed him that what was on his mantelshelf was of one of the rarest diamonds on earth. At this point the new owner of the house almost fainted. He informed the visitor that his back garden was filled with many like that. The story goes that the land the first guy sold in order to run off in search of diamonds was actually one of the largest diamond mines of its time. The irony of course is that he already owned it free and clear!

The moral of the story here is before you abandon your current career or organisation in search of another, make sure you have first exploited all the opportunities lurking within it. There was probably a very good reason you got into it in the first place. Have you gone as far as you can go? Have you delivered enough in the role or function to justify your experience in that area before you look to move on?

If you have analysed the situation and it is definitely time for a change, the first area to consider is moving to a different function within the existing company. The advantage you have here is that you can leverage your existing contacts and you should have a good understanding of how the business works.

Sometimes leaving the current organisation might be the right thing to do. This could be because progression within the company is limited. If you are working for a small company with only one FD and this person is relatively new in their role and performing it very well, chances are you may have to wait a long time to have a shot at that job. In this situation, the best thing to do once you are ready for the role is to jump ship.

Choosing the next role can be very challenging so it's worth putting things into perspective. Think about your long-term career aspirations and ask yourself which of the options will put you in the right direction. Sometimes this may require a short-term sacrifice. For example, if you have spent your whole career working for large companies and the outcome of your longer term goal setting is that one day you would like to be CEO of an SME or a startup, you would need to start making steps very soon that will stir you in that direction. This could mean taking a lower paid job in a smaller company but at least it gets you on to the right track for the long term.

An easy way to walk through options quickly is to put together a list of wants and don't wants. Reviewing your strengths and weaknesses can be very useful here. Ideally you should be looking out for a role that would maximise your strengths rather than expose you to your weaknesses, unless your area of weakness happens to be a critical skill for your aspirations. For example, if you have identified strong attention to detail as an area of weakness yet have an aspiration to become a finance director, you have a tough decision to make.

Time for action

At this point you should now have an idea of which option you choose to follow. It will most likely be one of those below so let's take them one at a time.

Staying with your existing employers and moving up the chain: I'm assuming at this stage you would have established that there are opportunities to move up where you are. There will be a number of scenarios to consider. Firstly, if the next role up is your manager's role then you will need to act with discretion unless you have a very good relationship with him or her and you are aware that he or she is about to move up. If this isn't the case then you're better off speaking with someone else you can trust, preferably someone outside your unit. You can also speak with someone in HR for example, but make it clear that this is confidential. If on the other hand there are a number of layers between you and your manager and you are looking to move up one level and still be reporting into this person, then speaking to him shouldn't be an issue. In both cases your first task is to understand the critical skills required at that level and compare that to yours. The gap you identify should form the basis of your development plan. The other area to also look at is your positioning. This simply means placing yourself where you will be noticed if one of the jobs you are after becomes vacant. This is easier if it's within your manager's organisation. If it isn't, you need to find a way to make yourself known to the other unit. Your manager may also be able to help; if not, find someone who can. In the meantime, your other priority is to ensure that you're delivering more than your current role requires. You have to demonstrate that you can do more than the job you've been given so others can see that you deserve a promotion.

Staying with your existing employers but moving to a different function: So you have decided it's time to move into a different function. This is trickier than the first option. Knowing your key strengths is critical here as you will need to find a way to demonstrate how you can put them to good use in the new environment. For example, if you're in finance wanting to move into sales you can use your strong communication skills and ability to explain complex financials to non-finance people as an applicable strength in sales where you will be relying on excellent communication skills to explain complex products to customers in a simple enough way so that they understand how the products will meet their needs.

Similar to the first option, you will need to have a good track record of delivering more than required. Very few will take a chance on a person without a good track record. Be proactive and find out the critical skills required for this role as quickly as possible and begin to make a case for how you can meet them. You should also get to know people in the business area you would like to join. Speak to someone doing a similar job to the one you're after to get an insider's view. Get introduced to the person you hope to be working for and don't be afraid to make your intentions known as long as it won't cause any problems with your manager. Look for a link between your current role and the new function and exploit that link first. Using the above example of wanting to move from finance to sales, if you haven't already, you can push to become the finance business support for the sales organisation. This will give you a fantastic insight into the sales organisation.

Moving to another company either in the same function or to change function: Hopefully before arriving at this option you have fully evaluated all internal options and reached the conclusion that you need to look outside. Sometimes this is the best thing to do. Look on the bright side, you will be giving yourself an opportunity to completely re-create and rebrand yourself. Exciting! Now let's examine the practicalities.

Moving to another company into the same function will be much easier than moving to another company and to another function. Much easier but not impossible. Depending on your level of seniority, track record and network, you may be able to command an external presence that will help you here. The best starting point is to assess who you know that can vouch for your performance and if they are now working for a company that you are interested in. This could be a former line manager or a former peer who may now be in a more senior role. If so, brilliant. If someone has worked with you in the past and it worked out well, chances are you will want them to work with you again. The other route is to use existing contacts to give you referrals into companies you wish to join. This isn't as good as the first but still better than cold calling. The final option you should explore is following the conventional route of using agencies and the internet to search for suitable vacancies. The more senior you get, the less fruitful this route will be for finding suitable roles.

This chapter has focused on you taking time out to reflect on what you want, understanding your current situation, coming up with options, selecting a course of action and going for it. This process does not necessarily need to be applied only when you need to change jobs but is also a useful way of developing your career whenever you get stuck on any challenges that you find difficult to find a way forward. Review the situation and decide on the ideal end state for that situation, establish your current position, evaluate your options and pick a path that will advance you toward the desired end state and go for it.

In the next chapter we will go through the early days, once you land that job, looking at how to make a strong positive impact within your first few weeks of joining.

#2
Be very clear on why you got hired

Most, if not all of us, will always remember the moment when we received that phone call to say we have been selected for the job and the company would like to make an offer. It is always a brilliant feeling. It means you pulled it off. They liked your CV, they called you for an interview and you smashed it! Or in some cases, you had a brief chat with someone you know, or a contact of a contact, and you impressed them and the person decided to shake hands with you and offer you the job. Either way it's a great feeling. Somewhere inside you feel like someone has just confirmed how wonderful you are! You may be new in your current role so will remember this more vividly or it might be a little vague.

Strangely, very few of us stop at this point to truly reflect on why we were hired, i.e. what skills and capabilities we demonstrated at the interview, or were sold by someone else on our behalf, that we will now be expected to put to good use to get some results. Whatever you do in these first few months will give people a perception of you that will last for some time so it is critical that you get off on the right start. If you have already been in your role for some time, that's fine. You can still implement what we're about to go through so please read on.

Every job is a problem that requires solving

A good place to start is the recognition that every role in any organisation is nothing but a problem that requires solving. To some extent, this statement may look like a generalisation. Some would argue that a sales job is a job created to pursue an opportunity to drive sales. Agreed. But if you don't achieve the sales that you need you will not be able to cover the costs of the business or make a profit for the investment. The problem here is that the company needs some sales to be made. The solution is the sales vacancy. If you got hired for this job, you were hired to solve the sales problem.

The vacancy may be due to a new role being created, a replacement for someone who left, or an addition to others already doing that type of role due to recognition that more hands are required. All of these are problems that need solving hence the need to get more people into the organisation.

Exercise 3

Take a few minutes to think about your current role. How well do you understand the problem that you have been hired to solve? This isn't as simple as reading the job description you were given at the interview, but understanding the repercussions if you don't do a good job.

What will happen if you screw up on the job? What could go wrong? If you're in sales, this won't just mean you miss your sales target, it could mean your whole department misses its sales target. Or even worse, your whole company. If you're in operations, what happens if you don't follow the health and safety measures correctly? Someone or you could get hurt. Maybe seriously hurt.

Make a note of what you would do differently the next time you're at work to make sure you are solving the problem you were hired to solve.

The piece you own lightens the load for someone above you

An organisation is a large collection of problems that need solving on a day-to-day basis. The organisation structure depicts a system where the person at the top has the largest problem and he or she breaks it down into smaller chunks and shares it out and the next person does the same. This process continues until you get to the lowest level of the organisation where each individual is allocated his or her own share of the problem. Solutions proposed or carried out then flow upward, not the other way round. It is important to understand this completely.

When you are given a job or task it inevitably will contain a measure of a problem that needs to be resolved and you will need to sort it out. The more you can do this, or even better, the more you do this and go back and ask for more and bigger problems to solve, the better you will do in your career. The more times you resort to reversing this flow, i.e. pushing problems back up the chain rather than solutions or proposals, the worse you will do in your career.

If you solve problems for your boss you will make his or her life easier and you will be rewarded for this. It also means more problems will be pushed downward to you and this is not a bad thing. It means you have established a reputation for delivering results so this trend is likely to continue. For example, the more problems you solve, the bigger and more complex the problems you will be asked to solve. At a certain point you will find yourself getting promoted when you reach that point where you are solving problems far bigger than your current role can handle.

The same with doing the opposite. The more you try to push problems upward, the more you're telling people that you are not capable of the job you've been given. At a certain point a correction will need to be made and you may find yourself either being demoted, or worse, dismissed.

I once worked with a consultant who was not only good at delivering on the project, he was also very good at soliciting problems from other consultants so he could share his insights on how he successfully dealt with similar scenarios for his clients. Eventually he was asked to set up and lead a small group of subject matter experts to be assigned to multiple projects. He later became the engagement lead for that practice, which did not come as a surprise to anybody. He started with solving problems for his clients on his assigned projects. He did this very well and started reaching out to others to help solve their problems, so essentially he was now solving bigger problems. His bosses recognised this and made him lead the subject matter expert group so he could solve even bigger problems and eventually promoted him to become the engagement lead for that unit − now he could solve much bigger problems. Naturally, his remuneration was increased accordingly to match the new size of problems he was solving for the organisation and so it goes on...

Exercise 4

What bigger problems can you solve in your current role? Take a few minutes and see what you can come up with. Perhaps this is something you can discuss with your manager today?

Someone thought you were right for the job

The good news is that before you got hired someone thought you were right for the job. They must have seen something in you: your experience, qualifications, way of working, attitude or some combination of these things. Enough to believe that you were right for the job. Enough to stake their reputation on you. Yes, this is exactly what someone does every time they hire you. This is also what you do every time you hire someone. You put your reputation at stake for them the same way someone else put their reputation at risk when they hired you or recommended you to someone else to hire.

Hopefully you see this as a welcome realisation. Someone thinks you're good. With that in mind, begin the job with the mindset that you can do it and prove that person right. Make them very happy to have recommended you so they will do it again and again in future.

A few years ago I was involved in interviewing a batch of candidates and was very impressed by a gentleman we will call Jack. Jack said and did all the right things during the half-day interview. He held the right posture, came across as very enthusiastic and answered every question at the interview very well. I wanted this guy on my team. Unfortunately, when I eventually hired him things didn't go as I had anticipated. The first day he arrived at the office he turned up 15 minutes late and didn't appear to think it was an issue. During our one-to-one briefing that morning he barely took any notes and later in the day clearly demonstrated that he should have as he kept asking the same questions. To the others in the team, he came across as overconfident and basically couldn't deliver as expected during the first three months in the role. In the end, after several coaching sessions, I eventually had to manage him out of the business. The whole process took nine months and a lot of pain.

A man who can read but doesn't is no better than a man who cannot read. When someone believes in you enough to recommend you or hire you for a role it is important you live up to that expectation. Some of us put in much more effort to pursue a role then take it as an entitlement when we land it. Never get complacent in any job you're doing. You have to constantly ask yourself and others if you are meeting expectations. Better still, strive constantly to exceed expectations so you can build in a comfortable buffer. Your reputation and the reputation of the person that hired you are at stake. Don't deliver on the job and you could put someone else's career on the line – they will never forgive you for this. Deliver and you've got yourself a personal publicist and sponsor for a long time to come.

The purpose of this chapter is to get you to understand why your role exists, why YOU got hired and to get you thinking of ways to ensure that you are meeting or exceeding expectations. The exercises should have helped to get you to come up with specific actions to take at work to address this. If you completed the exercises, you will find the next chapter even more useful as we look at the performance management process and how you can make sure you are delivering on the job quarter after quarter, year after year.

#3
Respect the performance management process – don't fight it!

So you've landed the job and you want to nail it. Great! To do this, you will need to make sure you thoroughly understand your organisation's performance management process. The larger your organisation, the more formal this process will be. For some, there will be a formal quarterly performance review process with informal monthly sessions. For others it could be twice a year with quarterly informal sessions.

During these review sessions your manager will provide a formal indication of where you stand, broadly on the basis of if you are below expectations, at expectations or above expectations. Naturally, this will have an impact on your remuneration and progression within the organisation. So whether you trust the system or not, like it or not, this is extremely important. If you believe you're a strong performer but keep getting a bad rating, that's a problem. It isn't something you can easily dismiss as it will have a very strong impact on how you are viewed by the next person you work for. The best thing you can do is listen to the feedback you have been given and address it. Understandably, you will have some instances of poor performance management from your manager, which is unfortunate, but remember this is your career. You are responsible for addressing this also. It is easy to blame it on your manager but don't let yourself fall into this trap. Take responsibility and ownership of the situation and deal with it.

A close friend of mine came to me once with a situation he had with one of his employees and wanted some advice on how to handle it. He had just been promoted into a role and inherited a management team that included a guy with a poor performance track record. During his first meeting with this gentleman (we will call Jim), Jim basically summarised that he had been unfairly rated for the past two years on his performance. My friend had looked into this and found very little evidence to justify the poor rating and most people he spoke with agreed that Jim was a strong performer and didn't deserve a poor performance rating. So I asked him what Jim had done about it for the past two years. Interestingly, not much apart from complain about it to others. Now from the evidence so far it appears Jim may have been badly treated. But who would you say is responsible for this over the past two years? Definitely not the line manager or the system – Jim is. I'm very certain if you look deeper into this case you will find out eventually that without question Jim is at fault. This will become much clearer by the time you finish this chapter so please bear with me.

Be clear on what's expected of you

At some point during the interview and hiring process you will no doubt have come across a job description for the role you are now doing. The job description or JD as its popularly known is a formal document that lists out everything that you are meant to be doing including what you are accountable for. But when was the last time you set eyes on your JD? Or when do you think was the last time your manager set eyes on your JD? I can guarantee that if you asked 100 people this question, fewer than 10 would have looked at their job descriptions a month after starting the job and even fewer for managers. There is a good reason for this. The purpose of the JD is to get the role approved by Human Resources so the hiring manager can go and find a suitable candidate. Once you are hired no one ever needs to look at this again. This may sound unfair but this is the reality from my experience. So how do you keep yourself up to date with what's expected of you? Ask your line manager. Not once but regularly. I would suggest that once every month you check in with your manager on what's expected of you and the extent to which you are meeting those expectations.

In your first week in any job, make sure you find time to meet with your line manager face to face if possible and get answers to the following five questions:

1. What are we (the organisation) looking to achieve this year?

2. What are you expecting me to deliver within my first year?

3. What are the key things you would like to see within my first three months?

4. What are the **immediate** priorities you would like me to attend to beginning **right now**?

5. Which one worries you the most?

The first question gives you the wider context in which you will be operating. This is very important for you to know as it gives you an opportunity to know what else you can bring to the table other than what you have been asked to do. Start thinking about this from day one. The second question helps you understand how you fit into this wider context. This should also give you enough parameters to build your strategy for the year. The third question is very useful to set your priorities. What is expected of you in the first quarter is priority number one for you. While it's important to know what's expected in the year so you can plan accordingly, knowing what's expected in the immediate quarter is vital. The fourth question provides you with an opportunity to make your first impression. Knowing the immediate priorities gives you a chance to deliver something quickly and send a signal to your boss and his or her line manager that you mean business. You want to let them know without any doubt that you are someone to watch (positively of course!). Finally, the fifth question is an opportunity to become your boss's ally immediately. What you are trying to find out with this question is what's currently keeping your boss up at night. Help him or her unburden themselves of this and you would have made an excellent start.

If you have been in your job for some time already and you didn't do this when you first started, that's okay. You can fix this very quickly. Book a meeting with your boss as soon as possible and ask him the five questions. The beauty of this is that those five questions are still relevant at any point in your career. You can start the conversation like this:

"Bob (your line manager), I've been thinking about how I make sure I'm delivering my best and thought it would be good to clarify your expectations of me. With all the recent things going on, can I just clarify precisely what you expect of me for the remainder of this year? What are the key priorities for this quarter?" And when you have had the discussion, you continue: "Thanks Bob. And finally Bob, which one of these things is most important to you, i.e. what's troubling you most right now that I may be able to take off your hands? I'm sure you have enough on your plate."

If doing what I have just described sounds uncomfortable to you, that's okay. It will be if you haven't done this before and it's a sign that you are on the right track. Uncomfortable usually means you are doing something out of your comfort zone and this is great. You are about to take things to a new level and this won't happen if you stay within your comfort zone. Depending on your relationship and track record with your line manager, he or she may also find this conversation weird and confusing, and may also be uncomfortable. This means they will be sceptical at first but I guarantee that if you deliver on the answers you get to these questions you would have succeeded in sending a clear message to your boss. Do it a few times and his or her impression of you will definitely change for the better.

The role of your manager

Your manager needs you to succeed because he or she has hired you and would get some of the credit for your performance. Your manager can also be your promoter as, like it or not, they will be in lots of meetings that you won't be privy to. They will also be in front of lots of people that you won't immediately have access to, and if you want these people to hear good things about you, you have to give your manager something good to say about you.

I'm sure there are some exceptions where a manager who is threatened by you will sometimes work against you but in the majority of cases your line manager wants you to succeed. This is because one of the fastest ways to rise in any organisation is by developing leaders within your teams who can take on bigger and bigger challenges. If you have strong leaders working for you, you too will be able to over deliver and unsurprisingly you will find yourself in a bigger role within the organisation. So do yourself a huge favour from day one. Get on the right side of your manager by exceeding expectations. Give him or her plenty of good stuff to say about you and keep doing it. Seize every opportunity to make their life easier and avoid every opportunity to make their life more difficult. Do this consistently and you can't go wrong.

Know how you will be assessed

Knowing what is expected of you is a very good starting point between you and your manager. You will need to know *how* you will be assessed and also need to clarify *what* you will be assessed on. In the earlier part of this chapter we talked about the five key questions to ask. The answers to questions one and two will need to be refined into quantifiable objectives which will form the basis of how you will be assessed. And this is your job not your line manager's. For example, your line manager might say the department is looking to hit a profit figure of X at a margin of X% and that you are expected to contribute to this. You need to make sure you are clear on how you will do this. What exactly is expected of you? If you're in sales, this means you will have a sales target so make sure you know what that is. For some other roles the link may not be as clear but it's just as important to clarify it. If you're in a support function like finance for example, your role might be to support and challenge the sales team to ensure they meet a particular target. This means you will be jointly responsible for that sales target with the sales team and so they need to know this. This way you will be seen as also having a stake in the ground and hopefully welcomed to contribute to the strategy and execution of the sales plan that will guarantee meeting that target.

It is also important to know what would be considered as exceptional performance so you can also strive for this. Once this is clear, then you need to agree monthly or quarterly milestones so you and your line manager can assess how you are doing toward the annual expectations. This way corrective action can be taken if you are going off track. In addition to what you are delivering on a monthly basis, it is also important to seek feedback on **how** you are performing the job. What behaviour is your line manager seeing that needs to continue and what behaviour needs altering?

Exercise 5

Reflect on the last performance management conversation you had with your boss. What actions did you put in place to address any feedback you have been given on areas to improve on? How would you say your performance has changed in relation to the feedback you received?

If you haven't received any such feedback, when did you last ask your boss for feedback on areas you can improve on? What about your peers, or your team, if you manage people?

Make a note of three people to ask this week for specific feedback on how you can improve your performance. Schedule some time in the diary with each of them to make sure you follow through with this action.

To summarise, it is important to know what is expected of you. If this isn't presented to you, ask for it. If you receive it and it isn't clear, seek to get clarification until you are totally certain. When you are clear on **what** is expected then seek to understand **how** you will be assessed. What specific outputs will be used to assess your performance? Is there a report that would be produced at the end of the year that will show this, like the sales report or P&L? Who produces this report and how frequently is it produced? Agree on milestones so you can check where you are regularly. What behaviours will your boss be looking for? Seek regular feedback from your boss and others so you know how you are doing against what's expected. Be very clear that this is a two-way process. This is **performance management** in action. Pursue it diligently and consistently and take corrective action where necessary and you will have no surprises. You will also find yourself excelling at what you do or recognising very quickly that you are in the wrong role so you can react swiftly and make the necessary correction. Either way, the most important thing is YOU will be in control.

Let's re-examine Jim's situation that I mentioned earlier. Do you now see that Jim would have had so many opportunities to address any perception gaps in his performance so as to avoid an end of year rating that came as a shock? And again, it was his responsibility to make sure his performance was properly managed, nobody else's.

In this chapter we've spoken mostly about you and your manager. But your manager isn't the only person that will have an influence on your career. In the following chapter we talk about others who also have a stake in what you do.

#4
There are others that matter, besides your line manager

It is extremely unlikely that your manager will be the only person you will come into contact with while performing your daily tasks, unless you work for a company that employs only the two of you. But I suspect this won't be the case for you. At the very least you will have others reporting into the same manager as you: your peers, your manager will be reporting into someone else and you will all be supported by human resources and finance teams.

You will also be supported by other teams such as IT and legal. Collectively, all of these guys can be defined as your stakeholders as they would be impacted to some extent by your actions. Now let's take each of these parties in turn, beginning with your manager's boss.

Your manager's boss

I remember being asked by my boss to prepare a presentation for her boss to give an update on a project I was leading on. She made me change the slides about five times and I remember thinking how pedantic she was. The day before the meeting, she took me aside to say how important this meeting was and that it would be a great opportunity for me to get noticed, so not to screw it up! She was absolutely right. The first chance you get to meet your boss's boss should be treated like your biggest job interview to date. Make sure you're on point on everything from your appearance, whatever material you take into that meeting and how you come across during the meeting.

This will be your opportunity to show an unfiltered version of your performance to the person who will need to approve your pay rise or bonus at the end of the year. It is also an opportunity for you to make your boss look good. After all, he hired you and if you come off well he'll get the credit for bringing in good talent. If you don't, he'll get the blame.

Your boss's boss will also be weighing you up as a potential successor to your boss, which means you could one day be working for him. If he or she sees potential in you, they will put you on their watch list. This means more opportunities will be created to bring the two of you together so your performance assessment can continue. You may soon find yourself having one-to-one meetings with this person. If this is the case, it means you're doing well. Keep making sure you are on top of your game for any of these meetings even if it's a 10-minute catch up. Never let your guard down.

Getting on well with your boss's boss also helps during performance rating time at the year end. It will be very difficult for your manager to score you low if his boss is singing your praises. That would be another way of your manager telling his boss that he is a poor judge of talent – whether he happens to be right or wrong is a totally separate matter. Similarly, you will be making your boss's job much more difficult if he wants to give you a fair rating and his boss thinks you're crap.

Building a good relationship with your boss's boss need not only be about you getting recognised. It can also help you with your career development. Whenever I get appointed into a new role I always seek time with my manager's boss to introduce myself personally and also to get his or her priorities for the organisation also. This wider view can help put things in perspective and also give you a broader understanding of the environment you are operating in. It also provides an opportunity for the person to get to know a bit more about you and most likely they will ask you questions too. Again, make sure you prepare thoroughly for this meeting. Make sure you have some great questions to ask and be prepared to talk about your most recent experience and how that would be applied to help meet the challenges the organisation is currently facing. Good questions to ask include:

- What do you see as the biggest risks facing the department right now?

- Where are the biggest opportunities?

- What are your expectations of me?

- What would success look like for you?

These are just examples to kick-start the discussion. Listen very attentively and follow the conversation in the direction that he or she takes it. You will make a better impression that way, rather than try to draw it back to the questions you prepared in advance. If you do that it will give the impression that you are not listening.

As time goes on, if you have built a good relationship with this person, you will also find that they will be someone you can call on from time to time for help. A word of caution is to not overuse this. Never go to your manager's boss for help if it's something your manager can help you with. If you do this repeatedly you will be giving his boss the impression that he is not good at his job. There will be times when it makes sense to escalate but do yourself a favour and check in with your boss first and make sure they are okay with it. In time you will get to know the things to take directly to his boss and what not to. The rule here is simple: if in doubt, ask your boss.

Your boss's peers

Your boss may be doing exactly the same job as his peers but covering a different area, e.g. he may be the Regional Finance Director for Europe in which case his peers will include Regional Finance Director for Asia, UK, etc. Or he may be doing a completely different job from his peers, e.g. he may be the Sales Director while his peers are the Finance Director, the Operations Director, etc. Regardless of which situation you find yourself in, it is imperative that you get along well with this peer group and their respective teams.

Each of these guys will have an input into the overall department's performance rating and will most likely have an opinion of you. During year end ratings reviews, my peers and I in turn present our suggested ratings for our teams to our line manager. He will then ask if anyone has any objections or was in support of the proposed rating. If everyone was in agreement things will go easily; if not, it becomes more challenging. We had an example of a guy where his line manager constantly gave a very good rating yet most people in the room thought he was an underperformer. Each quarter we will all settle for his rating being brought down to average. Clearly this guy was performing very well in the eyes of his line manager but this wasn't enough. It was equally important for him to perform well in front of the other line managers and this clearly wasn't the case.

The other thing to note is that one day you may fancy a change in roles, possibly to move to one of the other teams managed by one of your manager's peers. Naturally, your chances of success will be impacted by the perception this person has of you and also the feedback they would have received from their direct reports about you. This doesn't mean you won't get the job if they haven't heard or seen good things about you but it won't make the process easier.

Again, building a good rapport with these guys is not just about them giving you a good rating or increasing your chances of working for one of them in future. They are also people who can help you with your day-to-day challenges.

They can help you when you face difficulties interacting with their teams. It never hurts to be able to pick up the phone and call Mike if one of Mike's DRs is being totally ignorant! If Mike's experience of you is that you are always professional and easy to work with, he will listen to your complaint and support you accordingly.

Your boss's peers can also be good sounding boards for ideas. For example, if your manager has asked you to run a project on something and he happens to mention that another team have completed a similar project, it may be worth approaching that team. A good starting place is the team lead, i.e. your manager's peer. This person will most likely give you some good high-level tips and ask you to go into further details with the person they had working on the project. This could be a starting point to developing a good business relationship. As this relationship grows, you may find it easier to seek support from this person rather than your line manager as things evolve into a mentor/ mentee relationship. More on this in Chapter 7.

The Human Resources team

If there is one part of the business where you shouldn't make any enemies, it's Human Resources. Why, because HR is involved in all parts of the business and, more importantly, they own the performance management and reward system. They know about all the vacancies *before* they become vacancies and are involved in the final say of who gets the job.

Let's take the performance rating process first. Like the other two parties discussed above, HR would also have a seat at the table when performance assessments are being done. They too will need to be convinced of your performance especially if your manager is pushing for an above average performance. If they haven't seen anything exceptional from you or hear a number of others in the room singing your praises, they will be hard pushed to support your exceptional rating by your manager.

On progression, the advantage of having HR on your side is that sometimes they will have visibility of opportunities outside of your department and can put your name in the frame if you've built a good track record with them. This is particularly useful as, most times, by the time the vacancy becomes public, a shortlist of candidates would have already been selected.

One thing to note is that most people normally go to HR to ask for talented internal candidates whenever they are thinking of bringing someone into their teams. Wouldn't it be great if you are on HR's talented list? Imagine having HR as your own personal publicist!

Likewise, if you have a poor track record with HR, opportunities will disappear before you even get a chance to pursue them. Imagine going to HR to say you are considering approaching Jack for a role and you get informed that Jack has had several issues with each of his previous line managers and is currently involved in a grievance case with another member of staff but the details can't be disclosed for confidentiality reasons. How likely are you to proceed?

Putting your career rating and progression to one side, HR can also be a huge support in your day-to-day operation. If you manage a big team you may have a dedicated HR person assigned to you or have access to a team. I suggest you use this person as much as possible and not just to discuss people-related items when an issue materialises. Rather, try to get your HR business partner involved as much as possible in everything you do.

The Finance team

Like HR, the finance team are involved in every aspect of the business and are also seen as a trusted advisor. This means they also have a say in your performance rating and, most likely, your remuneration. Most senior business leaders see their finance person as their number two and main confidant. This means they are likely to be the first person they speak to whenever they need to make a decision about something. Having finance on your side means you are more likely to be favourably spoken about when it matters. This is a good thing.

With regards to your day-to-day operation, you will inevitably come in contact with finance very often. If you manage a large team, you will come in contact with finance whenever you need to hire someone to get their approval. Depending on your remit, you may also come into contact with finance to approve your business cases to invest in initiatives that you expect to provide a good return to the business.

Having a good track record will make it easier for you to move at pace when you want to get things through finance quicker in order to take advantage of a good opportunity. It can also make your life much easier. There is nothing as frustrating as going through a tedious and lengthy process to hire staff while the workload is piling up. If you have a track record of providing robust justification for your requests and you live up to the benefits you propose, you will become more trustworthy. If you are, people will spend less time scrutinising your requests. If you have a poor track record, e.g. your assumptions turn out to be materially different from the facts and you rarely deliver on the benefits you propose, then prepare for a very thorough review each time you raise a request, and justifiably so!

A word of caution

In reaching out to your stakeholder group for help, it is important that you strike the right balance between seeking help and being downright incompetent. There is a difference between asking someone to look at what you're doing to see if there are any gaps or aspects you hadn't thought of and telling them you don't know what to do. Do this repeatedly and it won't be long before your stakeholders start to question if this is the right job for you.

During conversations with your stakeholders, be careful about the information you share and with whom. Avoid getting personal about anyone and strive to remain professional at all times. People will form an opinion of you based on what you say about others. Avoid complaining even if you find a sympathetic ear. You will be labelled as a whiner. Try instead to discuss ways to fix the issue so you give the impression of someone who is always on the side of the solution rather than the problem.

No matter how well you get on with any of your stakeholders, especially your manager's boss, avoid saying anything negative to him about your manager. No one wants to hire a person who speaks negatively about their manager. This does not mean you never disagree with anything your manager says. Far from it. There is a difference between disagreeing with your manager and speaking negatively about him or her.

Exercise 6

Make a list of your key stakeholders and next to each, on a scale of 1-10, rate the relationship you have with each: 1 meaning non-existent relationship and 10 meaning very well established relationship.

If you have marked most of your key stakeholders at 7 and above, that's very good. It means you are well connected. If you have marked most of them below 7 and some even below 5, you have some work to do. Plan some time in your diary to meet with them and start to develop the relationship.

Key take out from this chapter is that you should become aware of your key stakeholders and invest the time to build good relationships with them. Make it easier to work and interact with this group and their teams. Also recognise that they are here to help you succeed in your role. Use them accordingly. In the next chapter, you will see why it is imperative to connect with a wider circle than your immediate team and how important it is to manage your stakeholder environment very well if you are to earn a reputation as a strong contributor in your organisation.

#5

Do more than your role requires... and then some

If you came into a role and did just what you were expected to do in that role, it is unlikely you will achieve more than mediocre performance. This is simply because if all you've done is only what's expected of you then you deserve to be recognised and paid what you were offered to begin with and no more. This might be okay for some people but shouldn't be enough for anyone who is ambitious and wants to climb up the corporate ladder.

The surest way to move up is by consistently delivering **more than** what is expected of you. This way you will naturally find bigger problems coming your way for resolution. The more you solve them, the bigger they will get. The bigger they get, the bigger the reward and also opportunities for promotion.

It is important that you don't just seek out to do this purely for your own gain; try to understand the level of accountability you have in your job.

To deliver more will require you to understand fully who you are accountable to. This isn't something most people think about. In any job you happen to be in, you will be accountable to your manager, anyone you manage, and the customers served not just by you but the entire organisation. You are also accountable to the community in which your organisation operates. And considering how much time you put into the work, you are accountable to yourself and, finally, your family. To all of these groups, you are accountable for making sure you do a great job, every day you show up for work.

Understanding this level of accountability when you go into any role should change your perspective completely. It will hopefully ensure you adopt the mindset of a good corporate citizen. This means from day one you will seek to understand the bigger picture of the environment you will be operating in. You will seek to understand the wider organisation's corporate objectives, strategy and purpose. Do you know your organisation's purpose? If the answer is no, I suggest you find out as soon as possible. What about the organisation's strategy and main objectives? Again, if you don't know, please find out and make sure you understand them.

You are not trying to find out the purpose and strategy for the sake of it. Find out so you can understand how your role fits in. You are a part of the organisation and are a part of its success or failure whether you understand it or not, or whether you like it or not. Understanding how you fit in and making sure you are contributing demonstrates that you care for the company's progress. Why shouldn't you? Would you rather your company performs badly?

Being a good corporate citizen also means you'll be on the lookout for what's right or wrong as you traverse your daily routine. More importantly, you will be willing to stick your neck out and intervene if you see something that isn't right. This doesn't mean you become a warden patrolling the halls but that you will be willing to raise an issue with the appropriate team to ensure someone does something about it, whenever you see something that isn't right, rather than ignoring it.

It also means you will be willing to help someone in need of assistance whenever you have the means. An example would be to take time out to help someone in operations put together a business case if you're from finance. While pulling together a business case with calculations of return on investment might seem easy for you, it could be quite complex for someone else, especially a non-finance person. This person doesn't even need to be someone within your department. If they need your help and you can provide that help, do it!

Expanding your remit and taking on good corporate citizenship will significantly develop your career in many ways.

It will broaden your circle of influence

Simply put, the more things you get involved in at work, the more people you will be dealing with. The more things you accomplish, the larger your circle of influence in the organisation. I was once asked to champion Health, Safety and Wellbeing for the unit I worked in and was told I only needed to attend four board meetings a year so shouldn't take much of my time, so I said fine I'll do it. I imagined myself sitting in a three-hour board meeting four times a year and naturally wasn't filled with excitement for what I had just taken on. When I started looking into Health, Safety and Wellbeing and my role as champion for the organisation I realised there was a lot more to it than four meetings a year. This is a serious subject, I thought to myself. The more I got into in, the more interesting it got. Eventually I created a governance team of more than 20 people across the globe discussing and running initiatives across the company to improve Health, Safety and Wellbeing for the 16,000 people who worked for the organisation. I could have stuck to simply attending four board meetings a year.

It will expand your network

If you stay within your immediate remit, you will naturally confine yourself to working with the same people that you come across in your day-to-day environment. Getting involved in things outside your remit will expose you to a wider network of people. I used to work with a guy I will call Mike while at Accenture and was amazed as to how many people this guy knew in Accenture. Whenever you faced any challenge, Mike not only knew who to contact, he was able to get them to agree to help regardless of how senior. I later discovered that Mike was in charge of volunteering and used to lead on several volunteering projects around the globe on behalf of Accenture and he did this in his spare time. Because of this work, Mike was in regular conversations with lots of very senior executives across the organisations so naturally he had access to them whenever he needed help on anything.

Your breadth of knowledge and experience will expand

Taking on a Health, Safety and Wellbeing championship role meant I ended up knowing more about Health, Safety and Wellbeing than the average guy in the company. It is one of those experiences you rarely come across yet it's fundamentally essential the more senior you get when you become responsible for a large number of people.

I encourage you to look within your department and volunteer to take on some additional responsibilities beyond your day job. Ask to be a representative for your department on something and work with other departments on it. You could volunteer to be the lead on reducing energy consumption across your department as part of a group initiative. A project like this will save costs, benefit the environment, increase your knowledge about energy consumption and get you known across the organisation. A win, win, win!

You will increase your leadership skills exponentially

Managing and leading a team of people under your remit is one thing. Leading a team of people across multiple teams where you have no direct authority, especially with some of them much more senior than you, is another thing entirely. Where you have direct authority you can set the priority and manage the person's performance accordingly. You can directly influence the outcome. You can basically tell people what to do. Reward them if they comply, penalise them if they don't.

It is a different story when the person you need to do a job is more senior than you or works for somebody else. Yes, you can go to their boss and convince them to force their teams to comply, but this rarely works. It rarely works because this person would have already set priorities for their teams and is unlikely to be hard on them for not doing what you've asked, knowing full well that it could negatively impact the work they have asked their teams to complete. Unless what you're asking them to do fits in with the agenda of that team's priorities.

Bottom line is that people will only do things for two reasons: because they want to or because they have to. The "have to" you can control if they work for you or if you are able to convince the person they work for that they have to do it. The "want to" is where true leadership comes in and this is usually where most of your effort will need to be put in the minute you step out of your immediate remit.

You will need to excite and energise people by connecting with something inside them that makes them want to do what you ask. This happens when you are able to define an end state, a vision, which is so compelling that the other person can't wait to see it and wants to be a part of bringing it to life. A person you connect with at this level will find time, regardless of how busy they are, to help you. This is true leadership in action.

Exercise 7

Can you come up with a list of three additional tasks you can volunteer to lead on in your team?

Is there something your boss has been talking about that needs to be done but hasn't yet been assigned to anyone? Perhaps you can volunteer for it before someone else snaps up the opportunity. Take a few minutes and see what you can think of.

If you can't think of anything, why not email your boss and tell him you would like to lead on something that would benefit the organisation in addition to your role and ask if he has any ideas. Make it clear that you would like to expand your contribution to the business. There are very few bosses that won't seize the opportunity.

Don't forget the day job

Now remember that while you are expanding your remit and taking on the good corporate citizenship, you are still responsible for your day job. Time and time again I have seen people get so carried away with other stuff that they forget to do the day job. Mike that I mentioned earlier on who was leading on volunteering could have easily been doing that job full time and neglected his main job but he didn't. Similarly with myself when I took on the Health and Safety role.

Truth is, some people get involved in the other stuff, e.g. volunteering, as a way to escape the boredom of their main job. If this is you I strongly suggest you deal with the boredom issue of your main job first before taking on anything else. It may be time for a job change. If you didn't already, go through the exercises in **Chapter 1 – It's your career**, and establish what you need to do next and act on it. Taking on a side role as a means to find job satisfaction will lead to you failing on the main job and that will get you into serious trouble. Over performing on the side role is unlikely to save you here as this isn't why you were hired. See **Chapter 2 – Be very clear on why you got hired.**

If you are taking on additional responsibilities for the right reasons, you will need to find a way to balance it all. Put the right governance in place where applicable and concentrate on leading. Put more energy into connecting with people's hearts and get more people involved so you are not doing it alone.

Using one of the examples above, like taking on the responsibility for reducing energy consumption across your department, rather than physically trying to turn off all the lights within your department every night before you leave, try running a series of workshops showing people how much energy is wasted when someone leaves a light switched on and goes home. Let them know how useful that energy could have been for a developing country experiencing severe energy shortage. This will get a large number of people across the team turning off lights, and you only had to give one workshop to influence that. Even better, speak to facilities and get the switches automated so they go off after a room has been empty for more than five minutes. These are very simplistic examples but hopefully you get the point.

Finally, be prepared to put in the hours when necessary. Building a great career will involve you working smarter and harder. This means you will need to put in the hours. This is a choice you need to make for yourself when you take on broader responsibilities bigger than your current role. Making sure you deliver on the day job is challenging enough and balancing it with other stuff will be even more challenging. It is also good to know when to stop so you don't take on too much and risk burning out. The end result is no good for you, the company or your family so it's not worth it.

Get the balance right. You can take on more and deliver more for your organisation. Put in the necessary effort to work smarter: connect with people and get them to help you deliver. Be the leader and make change happen across your organisation. Achieve the right balance and the rewards will follow.

If you have come to the realisation that you have only been focused on your day job and have not been contributing to the wider team then it's time to make some changes. It's time to reinvent yourself. The next chapter will explore this, looking at what to do when you start a new role.

#6
Seize opportunities to reinvent yourself

Some people are naturally gifted and seem to find themselves always at the top of their game in whatever they do, all of the time. This is very rare to find. For the majority of people, myself included, you'll find that performance levels tend to follow the shape of a curve, depending on the type of person you are. On a day-to-day basis for example, my performance starts at the peak in the mornings and starts to wane from about 1pm till 3pm then peaks again toward the end of the day. This means I do my best work in the mornings from as early as 7am till midday and again from about 4pm till about 7pm. This doesn't mean I can't function between 1pm and 4pm, it just means it isn't the best time for me to tackle my most challenging tasks. What is your curve like?

The same can be said of your career. Most people will be highly motivated during the first 12 months in a role. This is the period when you learn a huge amount, not just about the role but also about the company, and this is equally applicable for an internal move. Some people may even start to develop some mastery of the role during the 12 to 18 month period and this is a great time to be in any role. Some will carry this "high" beyond 18 months as they head toward the two year mark. At this point, you know what is required of you and have now mastered a way to navigate whatever challenges come your way. You would have established yourself as a high performer, in which case you are planning on taking things to the next level or moving to another role.

Every new role offers an opportunity for a fresh start

Starting a new role, whether internal or moving to another company, offers you an opportunity for a fresh start. It's day one, the score sheet is blank and everyone is watching. This is an excellent opportunity especially if you have just come off an unpleasant experience and this time you are going to do it differently. You are going to come in charged up and ready to sprint when you hear the whistle!

Start off right and be perceived as a top performer from day one and you will find it much easier to maintain this perception. Never underestimate the power of first impressions. Start right. Be clear on the problem you have been hired to solve. Do something extraordinary within your first three months. Remember to ask the five questions we went through in Chapter 3. For convenience I will repeat them below:

1.   What are we (the organisation) looking to achieve this year?

2.   What are you expecting me to deliver within my first year?

3.   What are the key things you would like to see within my first three months?

4.   What are the **immediate** priorities you would like me to attend to beginning **right now**?

5.   Which one worries you the most?

The answers to these questions will offer you a clear direction when you start your role. The answers to questions 4 and 5 offer a brilliant opportunity to make a good first impression. By asking these questions you will already be doing that to some extent as not many people do this when they start a new role. They just get stuck in and get to work and even if they do think about some of these questions, they make assumptions on the answers, but why assume when you can ask?

The other important thing to do is to have a game plan. I always have one whenever I start a new role. I'm sure you're wondering what a game plan is, so let me explain. A game plan can be described simply as your strategy to guarantee success in the job. Naturally, this plan will be fleshed out more and amended when you start the role as you will have a lot more information. This is the more theoretical definition of a game plan.

I define a game plan as an angle, YOUR angle, which you will bring to the role to GUARANTEE success in that role. This will be dependent on your own capabilities and, particularly, what you are exceptional at. How can you bring your exceptional skill to the role and in what way would you like to apply it?

For example, one of the roles I did in the past was an internal consulting role within central government. During the interview I was told that I would be given a cost efficiency target and would need to come up with ideas and a plan on how this could be achieved. The expectation was to conduct a value for money review and reach an agreement on what to do within six months and use the next six months to implement the plan. Having been working on cost efficiency programs for the previous two years, I had become very good at identifying opportunities and building a plan to implement and was achieving this, on average, over a 60 to 90 day period, and achieving savings of more than 20%.

My game plan, once I got offered the role, was to double whatever efficiency target I was given and come up with recommendations and a plan within three months, i.e.

half the time. I felt very strongly that if I achieved this, my success in the role would be guaranteed, plus I would have made an excellent impression within three months of joining the organisation. From the day I started, I had a laser focus on my game plan. Everything I did, from planning my day to how I communicated, even the way I dressed, was geared toward implementing my game plan. The result was that I identified more than double the efficiency target but I got the buy-in and came up with the plan within four months. This was still two months earlier than expected and I certainly succeeded in making an impression very quickly. One that lasted throughout the 20 months that I stayed with that organisation.

Exercise 8

Take a few minutes and grab your notepad and a pen. Can you articulate what your game plan is in a few sentences?

What can you start doing differently to guarantee success in your role?

Let everyone know there's a new guy in town and he means business

When you start a role, make a point to get noticed as quickly as possible – for the right reasons! In addition to implementing your game plan find a problem that you can apply your natural talent to very quickly. Again, you would have identified some good opportunities from the answers you get to the five questions. Pick which of the problems you want to solve, preferably one you know you can solve using past experience as your guide. Don't be afraid to also stretch yourself. **If you do only what you can, you will always know only what you know.** So find the problem and apply yourself to it and move at pace to bring about a resolution, quickly. To do this you will have to be at your best and bring your best thinking to the problem. Analyse quickly, take action and make an impact.

Another way to get noticed quickly is to make sure you make yourself available to help. Make a point of asking lots of questions and offer your assistance wherever you hear of something you can help with. Make a point of meeting people and introducing yourself to them and let them know the things you're good at as you listen to their challenges. For example, you can say something like: "I had the same issue in my last job. Would you like me to take a look? I have some time this afternoon."

Volunteer to take on the jobs nobody else wants and soon you will find they naturally gravitate to you. It would be what most of the others would be complaining about but not wanting to get involved in because it's too difficult. Speak to your boss and ask to have a go at it as you believe you'll be able to bring a fresh and unbiased perspective to the task. If you fail at it, you will get sympathy from others as long as you didn't go around bragging that you would get it done easily. If you genuinely applied yourself to it, your boss will praise you for your efforts. If on the other hand you succeed, you would immediately establish yourself as someone who gets results. Do watch out though as this could bring enemies as you would have succeeded in making some of them look incompetent!

Sometimes a bad rating can offer you an opportunity

If unlike the example in the previous section, you have found your first 18 months extremely challenging and have received an adverse performance rating, it could also offer you an opportunity to reinvent yourself. I know it's easy for you to take it personally and even go as far as feeling you have been unfairly treated; the best thing to do, however, is accept the feedback and drill into the root cause. I understand there are instances where an adverse rating is unjustified but in my experience the majority are not. If you're in this situation, this isn't the worst thing that could happen so take control of the situation rather than be victimised by it.

Feedback is a gift so start by going back to your manager to claim that gift you left on the table the first time. Schedule a meeting with him or her and, this time, really listen and find out exactly why you have been adversely rated. What are your development areas and what suggestions can he provide on how you turn this around?

Go back and review **Chapter 4 – There are others that matter, besides your line manager.** Who are your other stakeholders? What do they have to say about your performance? Chances are, if your manager is right about you, you will hear similar feedback from at least one other stakeholder. It is unlikely they are all wrong and you are exceptional!

Exercise 9

Look at the different parts of your role and examine to what extent you have met or are meeting the requirements. Don't only look at **what** you have achieved, also look at *how*.

- Do you engage well with people?

- Do you bring people along with you?

- How well do you keep your manager and your other key stakeholders updated on what you are working on?

- How regularly do you ask for feedback if your manager isn't forthcoming?

- How often do you ask your other stakeholders for feedback?

If necessary, revisit Chapters 2 and 3 to help with the questions below:

- Are you solving the problem you were hired to solve in its entirety?

- Are you abiding by the performance management process?

Make a note of what you will do differently when you return to work and put some time in your diary to ensure you follow through with the actions you come up with.

The answers to these questions will give you plenty of information on how to turn things around very quickly. Take the feedback you have received and the output from your own assessment and turn it into a plan. Tell your manager what you're doing and get his support. Most managers will be very supportive. Inform the other stakeholders also that you are putting a plan together to improve your performance and get their support.

Book a weekly review with your manager and start to tackle some specific areas that have been highlighted. Set some weekly objectives with clear deliverables and review this at the start and end of each week. This is a performance improvement plan in action! A good manager will instigate this but not all managers are good so don't leave it to chance, take control! It also looks good on you to be proactive here and start this process *before* your manager does.

To reiterate, set the objective, perform, seek feedback, take any necessary corrective action, set objective, perform, seek feedback, and so on. If you follow this process religiously you will be amazed at how quickly your performance will turn around. Eventually you will find yourself being identified as one to watch as you would have succeeded in putting yourself in an upward trajectory. But this will take some time so you need to be patient and persistent. Don't drop the ball on your performance improvement plan; deliver it and stay agile.

To summarise, it is important to see every new role as an opportunity to reinvent yourself. A new role gives you an opportunity to start afresh. Set the tone from the start and don't waste the opportunity to make a great first impression. Let everyone know you have arrived and you mean business. Keep doing the things that get you noticed as a top performer and you will remain a top performer.

In the next chapter we will talk about how to get some help to get you delivering top quality, consistently. You don't need to walk alone and this chapter will talk about the three main categories of people you need to advance your career at pace.

#7
Don't do it alone

It's amazing how often we prefer to tackle a problem ourselves and the last thing most of us will consider is asking for help. For some strange reason we see this as an admission of failure or defeat. For some, it's a confidence thing while for others it's sheer egotism. Whatever it is, if you find yourself with this "I need to do it myself" mentality then this chapter is definitely for you.

Let's begin by getting rid of this myth that asking for help is a sign of incompetence. Quite the opposite actually. When you haven't tackled a particular problem before, seeking help from someone who has is potentially the fastest route you can take to solving that problem. I have been in conversations several times with people who have expressed a desire for a particular profession yet have never considered looking for someone already in that profession to seek their advice on how to get to where they currently are. Surely the best person to help you get somewhere is the person who has already travelled the road you are about to travel and arrived at the destination in which you are headed, successfully.

There are several groups of people that can help in your career progression and for the remainder of this chapter I will focus on these three: coaches, mentors and sponsors.

Working with a coach

A coach is a person that can work with you on a particular challenge by helping you find the answers for yourself. The emphasis here is on helping you find the answers yourself rather than telling you what to do. As such, a coach doesn't need to have any technical experience in the area in which you need help but is able to use good listening and questioning techniques to get you thinking constructively about the issue and finding a way to move forward with solving that issue.

The other advantage of having a coach is that you become accountable to this person and sometimes that accountability to someone else rather than just yourself will keep you focused on completing the task even when it gets very difficult.

When you need a coach

The ideal time to use a coach is when you're stuck on a particular issue and can't find a way forward. This could be something you've just encountered, e.g. struggling to meet your target at work, or something you've been struggling with for a long time, like constantly feeling overwhelmed. An example of the former could be how you meet your sales quota for the quarter. You may find yourself struggling to come up with a plan to recover on your numbers. An example of the latter could be that you have just taken on some bigger responsibilities at work and are now finding yourself constantly working late and at weekends but still can't seem to get on top of things. You have tried several time-management techniques and read lots of articles and books on the subject. You have implemented lots of the suggested ideas but still can't see any improvement so, rather than continue, you find yourself searching for yet another time-management approach.

Another common issue you may be facing is deciding what to do with your career. Hopefully **Chapter 1 – It's your career** was useful to tackle this. If you're still struggling I suggest you work with a coach who will also be using a similar technique as outlined in Chapter 1. The difference is you will have someone there to guide you and hold you accountable to complete the task successfully.

How to get the best out of a coach

To make the experience with a coach successful requires you to be totally honest about the situation and open about how you feel during the coaching period. Be committed to resolving the issue and be prepared to take the actions you commit to at the time you agreed to do them. There is no point engaging in a coaching session if you can't follow through with the ensuing actions. Make sure you agree on the appropriate medium and time for the discussion. Try to have the discussions face to face wherever possible and be on time so you improve your chances of being emotionally, mentality and physically ready for the session.

Have a pre-meeting or discussion with the coach first to find out more about them and to ensure that they are someone you can work with. If you don't feel comfortable talking to the person for whatever reason, look for someone else.

Benefits of using a coach

Objectivity – Because the coach is not emotionally connected to you or the issue, they can remain 100% objective. It's an entirely different situation than if you were talking to your boss for example.

Accountability – Typically each coaching session will end with you committing to taking certain actions before the next session. The mere fact that you commit to these actions to the coach and you will meet them by a certain date increases the likelihood of you carrying out those actions significantly. It's like what happens when your boss books a catch-up session with you on a project you're working on. You find yourself chasing as much as possible to bring the project up to date before the meeting.

Confidentiality – You may not want to expose some of your vulnerabilities at work and may prefer a safer environment to open up completely about your issue. A coach can guarantee total confidentiality and provide you with that safe environment to facilitate the discussion. An example of this is if you start to get the feeling you're in the wrong job. Working through this with a coach will give you a safe environment to explore all the options before you approach your manager or HR.

Where to find a coach

Before you start looking for a coach it is worth understanding the type of coach you need. The main types are business and executive coaching, personal or life coaching, and career coaching. Business and executive coaching will focus on developing the skills required to function and lead in the workplace, while personal or life coaching will focus on helping you understand your inner values and how to align them with your objectives and behaviours. Career coaching will focus on building the career path that is right for you.

Once you have an idea of what you want, the following avenues will help to find a coach:

Referrals – Ask around and see if any of your friends or colleagues have used a coach that they would recommend. See if they can introduce you to the person. You can then make contact and ask if they offer the type of coaching you require.

Professional organisations – You can use professional organisations like The International Coach Federation, European Mentoring and Coaching Council, and the Association for Coaching. Each of them will have affiliated members who provide professional coaching and should be able to provide you with a profile of each of their coaches.

Google search – A search of Google will reveal thousands of pages of information which will require plenty of time to go through. The clearer you are about the type of coaching you need, the easier it will be to narrow your search.

Once you have identified a coach, look at their level of coaching experience and relevant business or industry experience. Most coaches would argue that they don't need any experience in your industry to coach you as coaching is a process of helping the individual find answers for themselves. This is true, as mentioned earlier in this chapter. My personal experience of coaching suggests that sometimes it helps to have someone with some relevant business or industry experience.

For example, there was a point in my career where I got completely overwhelmed with my work and my private life. I was in a constant state of exhaustion which eventually led to stress. I had to-do lists coming out of my ears at home and at work and found myself falling behind on so many things. At that time I was running a global engineering team spread across more than 30 countries and had set up a charitable foundation focused on improving the lives of young children around the world. During my Google search I stumbled across a coach who had experience at senior levels in international roles leading large teams across multiple regions over a 20-year period. I contacted him and after our first conversation hired him to coach me for three months. It was clear to see during my coaching that he knew where I was coming from whenever I tabled my challenges because he had experienced similar challenges.

This doesn't mean a coach without relevant industry experience will be less successful than one that has, but in my opinion, it doesn't hurt. So my suggestion is that, wherever possible, you seek someone with some relevant experience. Have a trial session first to make sure there is a good rapport between the two of you before you commit to a coaching arrangement.

Working with a mentor

While in coaching we argue about whether the person needs relevant business or industry experience or not, in the case of a mentor this is absolutely necessary. The role of a mentor is to guide you through a problem or situation that they have experienced in the past and dealt with successfully. Essentially, the role of a mentor is to use their experience to help you get to an answer quicker than you would have done yourself, by providing you with some guidelines. This way you have the opportunity to gain directly from their vast experience. A mentor will tend to be someone more senior and more experienced than you in their career.

I have been extremely fortunate in my career to have been mentored by some very influential people that I have learned a lot from. I have discovered that the higher I go up the corporate ladder, the more I need one to guide me as the organisational issues I become responsible for get bigger and more complex. For this reason, I continued to work with mentors both within and outside my organisation. I tend to seek mentors with a considerable number of years of experience beyond mine and who are much more senior.

Why you need a mentor

There are several reasons why you will need a mentor and it is worth reflecting on these before you go looking for one. Most of the reasons will depend largely on your own individual circumstances. What follows is a summary of my top three reasons why you need a mentor.

Finding your next role – The more senior you get in an organisation, the less likely you are to find suitable roles advertised in your corporate vacancy list without a shortlist of people already earmarked for that role. One of the first things I do when I need to hire someone is contact people within my network to ask if they know of suitable candidates. Having a more senior and connected mentor will give you access to these roles before they make it to a vacancies notice. Most senior roles never make it there. Even better if your mentor is willing to personally recommend you for the role, depending on how impressed they are with you.

Access to their network – In most organisations, large ones especially, knowing the right "go to" person and having access to them can make the difference between success and failure in your role. Having a more senior mentor can expose you to a much wider network. Your mentor can help you tap into it by introducing you to the appropriate individuals whenever the need arises. I will cover more on networking in Chapter 9.

An invaluable sounding board – I'm sure we can all recall times when we're faced with issues we don't feel comfortable raising with our managers. This is usually because we don't want to be seen as incompetent or sometimes because we don't feel comfortable talking to the boss about it. This is another area where the help of a mentor can be invaluable. Some people may find it even easier with an external mentor who is unlikely to have any links with their current organisation.

How to find a mentor

So you know you need a mentor, now how do you go about actually finding one? For some this is easy. They find someone they like or admire and they go for it. For those who find this difficult, let me attempt to provide some guidelines to overcome this challenge.

I work with several mentors at any given time. Some I have had for years while some I work with for a specific period or a specific challenge after which we both move on. In some cases, the word mentoring never got discussed, the relationship just evolved into a mentoring one. In other cases, I have gone out looking specifically for a mentor. I have found both paths equally rewarding. Below I outline three simple steps to follow to find your ideal mentor.

Step 1: Decide what you need from a mentor – Before going out to seek a mentor you should first ask yourself what it is you are hoping to achieve from the relationship. What do you need most at this point in your career? In the previous section I talked about why you need a mentor, e.g. to help you find your next role, increase your network, or someone that can help you deal with the day-to-day challenges in your role. It is possible that you can find one person to do all three but you will have a much better result if you are clearer about your priority when you decide to find a mentor. This will increase your chances of finding the most suitable person.

Step 2: Identify who your mentor should be – Once you are clear about what you need from a mentor, it becomes easier to identify who to approach. If you have just taken on a new role, let's say in marketing and it's your first big role, you may decide you need a mentor to guide you during your first year in the role. Ideally you will need someone very senior in marketing with years of experience within or outside your organisation.

Or take another scenario. You may decide that having done your current role for a number of years it's time to move on to something different, say from finance into operations. In this case you may decide you need a mentor in operations or, more specifically, someone who has successfully moved from finance into operations.

Once you are clear about what you want, jot down as many names as possible of people you know fit the criteria. If you don't know anyone, ask people around you. Use LinkedIn to look up career profiles within your contact lists or those of your friends and colleagues. Look at organisation charts within your current organisation and look up the career profile of the person doing the roles you aspire to do. You should also ask your manager and your key stakeholders if they know suitable candidates. This way you can tap into their network, which will ensure you cast your net very widely.

Step 3: Approach your potential mentor – This is usually the most difficult part especially if you identify someone that you have never met before. Sometimes approaching the most senior people in an organisation can be very daunting. Like approaching the CEO of Apple and asking if he can be your mentor. From experience, this needn't be and actually I have found people of this calibre to be most willing to help and very engaged on the subject of mentoring. They know too well that they couldn't have reached where they currently are without some help along the way. The real challenge is how you get access to them.

So what's the best strategy to reach out to this group? An email like: "Hello John, I work in IT and am thinking of moving to sales and wanted to ask if you will be my mentor" might work but the chances are very slim, especially if John doesn't have a clue who you are. To increase your chances of success, find someone you know that knows John and ask them to make a personal introduction. An alternative approach if you don't know anyone that knows

John is to find someone at John's level in the organisation who can speak to John on your behalf. John is more likely to respond to someone at his level that he may know personally or have heard of.

The other route I have exploited in the past is to go via the person's personal assistant. This is the person who manages the diary of the executive you are trying to meet and, more importantly, someone who knows the exec very well. A phone call to them can be useful to find out a bit more about the person and whether they are someone who is willing to take on a mentee, etc. The assistant can also ensure you receive a reply from the exec and, if they agree to mentor you, will make sure you get some time in the diary. You will be amazed at how easy it is to get face time with a very busy senior executive once you build a good rapport with their assistant!

While the majority of people go through their career successfully without ever using a coach, it is extremely unlikely they would have been successful without ever working with a mentor. If you are currently not working with a mentor, I suggest you follow the above steps and find one very soon.

Working with a sponsor

Working with coaches and mentors is more common these days but very few people are aware of this third category of people that can help. You probably already have sponsors but you just don't identify them as such. So who is a sponsor as far as your career is concerned? A

sponsor is someone who actively promotes you within the organisation and will sing your praises whenever they have an opportunity to do so. They will mention your name in conversations that happen at very senior levels within the organisations with the objective of making sure you are considered for the big jobs when they become available. Put simply, their role is to get you moving up the career ladder in the shortest possible time as long as you keep delivering on the job.

The interesting thing about sponsors is that we don't go looking for them. They find us. By this I mean a sponsor tends to connect with you if they've worked with you in some capacity and have had an opportunity to see what you can do and get on well with you. They see the potential in you sometimes even when you don't. As a result, they can't help but sell you constantly across the business. Sponsors tend to be very senior people in the organisation, so naturally the more they talk about you, the more likely you will be considered for bigger roles. The other advantage is the exposure they will have to what's happening in the organisation and their direct involvement in creating the big job opportunities that you will be after.

How to make sure you have a sponsor working for you

Compared to finding a coach and a mentor, finding a sponsor is more difficult. This person has to believe in you and want to see you move up the career ladder as quickly as possible. In addition, this person will be willing to invest their own time and resources into making this happen.

One angle to explore is to work with a mentor on your career development and stay working with them over a long period. Doing this will inevitably turn your mentor into a sponsor as they will get to know you better over time, and if they start to see potential in you they will inevitably begin to sponsor you and actively sell you across the organisation.

Exercise 10

If you don't currently have a mentor, how many people can you immediately think of that would make a great mentor to you?

Next to each name, state if they are someone you know or know someone that does. Next to each name, write down how you think each of them can help you with your career.

Rank them in order of who you would like the most to be your mentor. Pick the top two and develop a plan to make contact following what you have just read above.

If you are already working with mentors, make a list of your mentors and study this list carefully. Can you identify one of them that is actively sponsoring you? If not, which of these mentoring relationships could you develop into a sponsorship?

What actions do you need to take to move this forward? Make a note of them and create a calendar entry with a description of the next action you need to take on this, to ensure you follow through.

This chapter has concentrated on outlining the help you can get from others and how to go about getting that help. In the next chapter I will return to you and talk about how improving your communication can help propel your career upward at pace.

#8

Become an excellent communicator

Communication is the lifeblood of any organisation. Messages have to be passed down from top to bottom and vice versa. Strategies and objectives are set at the top and need to be cascaded right down to the front line. Feedback on events needs to be passed back up the chain. Either way, it is vital that the key messages intended are successfully delivered and well understood by the recipient.

So wherever you happen to find yourself in the organisation hierarchy, your communication skills are important. If you aspire for leadership roles, it is imperative that you continue to sharpen and improve your communication skills. A good rule of thumb to remember is that:

The responsibility for getting the message across rests with the **"communicator"** *not the* **"communicatee."**

Simply put, you are responsible for making sure your message is well understood by your intended audience. You should never blame the other party for not understanding you. If they don't, you either didn't send your message via the right medium or it simply wasn't clear enough.

In this chapter I will cover communication in three areas: firstly in speaking, with a focus on public speaking; secondly in writing, looking at one of the most common forms of written communication in business today, email; and thirdly in messaging, focusing on how to get your message across more clearly and concisely, every time.

Speaking in public

If you aspire to lead people in any setting, be it public service or business, it is inevitable that you will find yourself needing to address large numbers of people from time to time. For the purpose of this section, I define public speaking as speaking to groups of people of 50 or more. This could be people that you know personally or not and could all be within your current organisation or not. Speaking in public happens to be included in the top five fears of most people around the world so I thought I would start on this evidently difficult subject. Some people even rate public speaking as more scary than dying! This is uncomfortably true.

If you are fortunate to be one of the few that find speaking in public easy, great for you. I will still encourage you to keep reading as you will find some useful tips to improve your craft. This is one area in business where you can't be too good. If on the other hand you are like the majority of people who find speaking in public challenging, then this section, actually this whole chapter, is definitely for you.

As a leader, you will find that one of your key roles is to ensure that your team is aligned to your organisation's mission and objectives and one way to do this is to communicate this message continually to large groups of people across the organisation. It is important that people are clear on the direction in which to go and need to be energised and motivated to want to go in this direction. While there are other ways you can deliver your message successfully, it will be difficult to avoid speaking to large groups of people entirely. This shouldn't fill you with fear as the good news is, like most things in life, if you are not good at something, you can learn it.

How to get good at public speaking

There are tons of books written on the subject of public speaking and what I present here is by no means exhaustive, so I encourage you to read further on the subject. For convenience, I have outlined some of my top tips on how to improve your public speaking skills.

Start with the basics – Most people get so nervous that as soon as they get on stage they jump into the speech they prepared. They immediately start talking and some even start before they get on the stage. This is usually due to nervousness and though they may try to portray it as bravado, it rarely comes across that way.

It is much better to wait till you get comfortably on to the stage, take a deep breath and pause while you take in the audience for a moment. Pick someone in the audience and smile at them, and then start. This will demonstrate that you are in control. Start with the basics, like thanking the audience for the opportunity to speak, introduce yourself and say what you plan to cover and why it is relevant for the audience. This will help you relax and you will also gain some respect from the audience for your courteous approach.

Speak slowly and don't be in a rush – Believe it or not, most people want to hear what you're saying so speak slowly and clearly and try not to be in a rush. Pay attention to the points you are making and make sure they are coming across as intended. Listen to yourself as you speak and play out your sentences. I have listened to people give speeches and start explaining something and very abruptly switch to something else. If you slow down and listen to yourself as you speak, you will know precisely when to move on to the next item.

Prepare well in advance – There are several reasons for speaking in public: to inform, to entertain, to influence, to inspire and motivate, or to sell. Sometimes it's a combination of these. It is important to know in advance what you intend to achieve and plan your message accordingly. It is also a good idea to take some time to learn about the audience. What would they like to hear and how can you incorporate that in your message. I will expand on the aspect of messaging later.

Being well prepared will help you be more relaxed when you come on stage and you will feel more in control. If you are not well prepared, you will need to be extremely good at public speaking to pull it off. You will still risk coming over as an amateur in your field if your content is inconsistent even though your delivery is flawless, so do yourself a favour and prepare thoroughly.

Make eye contact – As you speak, look across the audience and pick a person in a cluster and make eye contact. Hold their gaze for a few seconds as you make a particular point, then move along to the next cluster and do the same. Try to move your gaze in this manner across the entire audience one cluster at a time and repeat. This way you are not focused on only one part of the audience as you will disengage the other part. Avoid holding your gaze with one person or cluster for too long as it will get uncomfortable and awkward, so keep moving gradually across the audience.

Join a speakers club – For those who cringe at the thought of speaking in public, joining a speakers club is probably the best way forward. Here you will have an opportunity to meet lots of others like yourself and be part of a support network. During a typical session you will each be required to stand up and speak about anything. This practical approach is one of the best ways of helping you break your fear of public speaking.

Seek opportunities to speak in public – Finally, if you want to really get good at speaking in public then you should proactively find and create opportunities to do so on a regular basis. Nothing beats practice. The difference between this and the speakers club is that this will be without the support group and at some point you will need to get into the real world. Finding opportunities to speak in public should be easy as most people would rather not do it!

Write clearly and concisely

We looked at speaking in the previous section; now let's turn our attention to writing. The typical forms of writing in business include reports, presentations, memos, letters and emails. Like public speaking, numerous books have been written on reports and presentation writing, so I would encourage you to find some if you wish to improve in this area. For this section, I will concentrate on emails.

Email has become the number one mode of written communication in business today. We carry our email inboxes on our desktop, tablet and smartphones so are constantly communicating. This carries with it an element of risk as we sometimes end up sending emails that we shouldn't have or at least should have worded differently. For example, you are on a flight and the crew have announced preparations for take-off. You decide to check your emails quickly and you read an annoying email that you feel compelled to respond to. In that emotional state, with the additional pressure of needing to type quickly and send before the plane takes off, how likely are you to send the appropriate response? Surely you would have been better off waiting till you land or even sending the email in flight mode without the time pressure.

When we are caught up in the day-to-day challenges of our busy schedule, it is easy to forget the importance of a properly worded written communication. We switch from a quick email to a friend or colleague to confirm when we're meeting for a drink after work to an email to a customer responding to an earlier complaint, then back to an email to a colleague confirming that you can make the team's quarterly meeting and on to an email chasing a supplier for a delayed delivery. If we are not careful, you can see how easy it is to use the wrong tone in an email and get the message completely misunderstood.

Most people just start writing an email or replying to an email without stopping to think of what message they wish to convey. They would simply type the message, read through it quickly, checking for mistakes, then hit the send button. Some don't even read through it before sending. I receive an average of 300 emails a day and normally respond to a quarter of that because the majority of emails are for information only, in which case I only need to file them away. Some are junk that simply need to be deleted. Either way, having to respond to about 75 emails a day with no more than a few hours to spare would give about two minutes per email. Understandably, being clear on what you need to say, drafting and reading through your email before sending in two minutes will be challenging.

If you choose to rush this by not being clear on what your email message is and not reading through it before sending, the result is usually more emails. More emails because your message wasn't understood so the person comes back with an email like: "Sorry, not sure what you mean by…" or something like: "You've sent it to the wrong person," or worse still, they don't respond so now you have to chase them with another email.

So how can you alleviate this dilemma?

There are several ways you can manage this situation better. The most effective is to do things that reduce the volume of emails you receive while becoming more efficient at handling the emails that you do receive. You might be wondering why this is relevant under a section on becoming an excellent communicator. Well one of the reasons people communicate badly is due to time constraints. Emails are one of the great time stealers in the workplace today, so attempting to master some good habits to reduce the number of emails you receive in the first place will create more time to deal with the more important emails which need to be properly crafted.

Let's talk about how to improve your email communication and improve the effectiveness of the emails you send.

Ways to make sure you hit the mark with your emails

Make sure you are clear on what you want to achieve. Most people start writing an email without even thinking about why they are writing the email. Sometimes they are prompted purely by the email they received, sometimes not. Before you start typing, ask yourself the purpose of the email. Is it to inform someone of something? Or to influence them to your way of thinking? If so, what would you like the recipient to do as a result of reading your email? For example, look at the following two emails:

> "Just a quick note to let you know that the 'all team call' will be on Friday, June 17 at 2pm. Please speak to Angela Baker, our communications lead, to get more information."

> "Just a quick note to let you know that the 'all team call' will be on Friday, June 17 at 2pm. You will need to register to be able to join the call. To register, please send an email to Angela Baker, our communications lead, stating your full name and department, thank you."

In the first example, though it states that you should speak to Angela Baker to get more information, it doesn't say why you would necessarily need more info. It also sounds as though the email is merely for information only so you are probably likely to read and delete the email without taking any further action.

In the second example, you can see that there is a clear call to action: "You will need to..." as opposed to the casual statement in the first example "... to get more information."

Always read through your emails before you send them. This is particularly important to make sure what you were thinking in your head has come through in your draft.

Sometimes just one incorrect word can completely change the tone and meaning of an email.

Keep your message succinct. Try not to go beyond two or three paragraphs if you can help it. Aim to ensure your email doesn't stretch beyond one screen view to avoid the reader needing to scroll downward to finish reading it. Most people would hesitate to read your email if they see that it goes beyond one page view.

Tips on how to reduce email traffic and process your inbox more efficiently

When sending an email, take a minute to ensure you are sending it to the right person. Always consider carefully whom you choose to copy. Why are they being copied? Do you need a response from them or is it purely for information? The more people you address your email to, the more responses you are likely to get, and most of it may be unnecessary.

Avoid using "reply all" whenever possible. Nothing generates multiple emails as much as this does. If you use "reply all" and you are only really communicating with the sender, you will encourage others to do the same. You will then have the joy of having to read or at least open the emails of almost everyone else in the chain. You choosing not to use "reply all" isn't a guarantee that others won't do it but you will reduce the likelihood and certainly reduce the amount of unnecessary emails in somebody else's inbox!

Try to process an email once you open it. Avoid opening and closing emails as this can be a huge time waster. For example, if you open an email and it's something you are being informed about, make a decision right there and then on if it's an email that needs to be deleted or filed for future reference. If it's one to be deleted, delete it straight away. If it needs to be filed, then file it in a place where it can be quickly retrieved when necessary.

If the email received requires you to take action and it will only take a few minutes, act on it immediately if you can and either delete or file away the email. If it will require you to take much longer than a few minutes, find a space in your calendar when you can deal with the email. Create an appointment and place a copy of the email in the appointment. You can then store the email in a folder specifically named for actions that require longer to act on. You can delete the email from this folder when you get to the appointed slot and successfully carry out the required task.

Present clear messages

The first two sections covered spoken and written communication mediums. For the final section of this chapter, we will look at the message itself regardless of the medium. As mentioned at the start of this chapter, the responsibility for getting the message across rests with you, the "communicator," not with the "communicatee" or recipient. So if your recipient reads your email or hears you say something and doesn't understand it, it means you haven't communicated the message clearly enough or perhaps you haven't used the right medium.

For a message to get across successfully the following components need to be in place.

The **purpose** of the message needs to be known upfront. What is it that you are trying to convey and what reaction do you want as a result?

It also helps if the **needs and wants of the recipient** are known. What would they like to hear in relation to your message? Will they be pleased or angered by it, or indifferent? Anticipating this will help you with the right choice of words and style.

If your message is a call for action, you need to state clearly not just what needs to be done but how and by when. This should be specific not implied. See example in the above section.

Start with the main message of your communication then go through the details leading up to this afterward. Most people tend to do the opposite. They go into a long narrative and put the big bang message close to the very end. The problem with this is that most people won't get to the end of your communication so will miss your message entirely. For example, which of the following directions are you likely to listen to with full attention?

> **Example 1**: "Drive along this road heading east, take a left as soon as you come to the first roundabout, then turn right and follow the road to the end, then at the first set of lights, take the

right turn…" and so on, then finally end with: "There you will find a restaurant that serves the best Thai food you've ever eaten!!"

Example 2: "I heard you love Thai food and I know just the place. Let me give you directions. Drive along this road heading east, take a left as soon as you come to the first roundabout, then turn right…" You get the drift.

In the first example, it would be difficult to continue listening to the directions and retaining the information when you don't know where it's taking you to or whether it's a place you want to go in the first place, so naturally you would either switch off or interrupt and ask the person why they are giving you directions in the first place. While in the second example, if the person is interested in going to dinner and happens to love Thai food, they will have your full attention after the first sentence and will most likely retain all of the necessary information to ensure they can find the restaurant afterward.

#9
Master the art of networking

Lots of people talk about networking. Networking events are held at several bars across London almost every evening and many people attend to meet likeminded individuals, sometimes more for personal reasons than professional. So what is networking and why are so many people obsessed by it?

Let's start with the definition. Networking from a people perspective, not to be confused with computing networking, when searched in Google returns the following definitions:

"Networking is a socioeconomic business activity by which business people and entrepreneurs meet to form business relationships and to recognize, create, or act upon business opportunities,

share information and seek potential partners for ventures."
– **Wikipedia**

"Business networking is leveraging your business and personal connections to bring you a regular supply of new business."
– **Entrepreneur.com**

"Creating a group of acquaintances and associates and keeping it active through regular communication for mutual benefit."
– **Business dictionary.com**

You can see from the above definitions that networking carries a wide range of meanings from one person to the next. But let us consider some of the key points.

Key points to pull out from these definitions include:

- The intention to gain something from joining

- Like-minded people getting together

- The expectation of an ongoing relationship

My definition of networking is as follows: a process of meeting and building long-term fruitful business relationships with a wide range of professionals that you either do business with now or plan to at some point in the future.

Why networking is imperative in business

Firstly, let's look at why it's important to network within your existing organisation.

Connection to the wider business: The more people you know in your organisation, the more opportunities you have to learn about what is going on in other parts of the business. This will help you understand how your unit fits in with the wider organisation's goals and objectives. This will also help you identify where you can add more value than your role requires, as discussed in **Chapter 5 – Do more than your role requires.**

Access to real time information: Organisations are generally hierarchical especially the larger ones. This means news tends to travel across the top layers before traveling downward. So things going on in other units that you need to be aware of will be communicated by the head of other units to the head of your unit, who will then decide how much should be cascaded down, before you eventually get to hear some of it. If you already have good contacts in other units, you will have the opportunity to find out things much quicker and usually in more detail than by the time your unit head cascades this. This can sometimes give you an advantage over your peers.

Help with resolving issues: It's usually much easier to navigate issues that can be resolved within your unit that don't require input from other units than when it involves other units. This is only natural since you work more closely with people within your unit so generally know who you need to speak with to resolve issues. Also, if things get difficult your unit head can step in and help close the issue. When a problem involves other units, it is very helpful to have good relationships with the other unit heads that you can call on.

Access to opportunities: The contacts you have in other units will help make you aware of opportunities coming up in those other units before they become open to everyone. The more contacts you have, the wider your access to opportunities when it's time for you to move to another role. Most times in organisations you find that by the time a vacancy appears in the public domain, the candidate for that role has already been identified. This means you need to be in the running for that role well in advance if you are to have a real shot.

Why it is important to network outside your organisation

Networking outside your organisation provides similar benefits as networking within, with the added bonus of access to a much broader landscape.

Access to information: Here you have an opportunity to network across the industry and understand what's going on with other organisations and how that links with yours.

Access to external opportunities: Similarly, the wider your network, the more opportunities you will be aware of and can take advantage of whenever you consider making an external move. If you rely solely on searching for vacancies online or via newspaper ads, you will be limiting your chances significantly. Much more effective to already be on the mind of the person who has just created a vacancy in their organisation, well before any ad is placed in the public domain.

Advice you can get: Sometimes when working on a project, it is worth getting an external perspective for benchmarking purposes. This can be extremely difficult if you don't know anyone within the organisation that you wish to get information on. You don't even need to know the right person as long as you know someone that can help you identify the right person and, even better, introduce you to that person.

How to network

So you understand you need to network, great! So how do you network? I hear lots of people ask. Networking comes easy to some people but not to others. We all know someone who always seems to know everyone. They are the types that walk up to people easily, introduce themselves and immediately engage in conversation. For some of us, this isn't so easy. But this isn't all it takes to network.

Meeting someone is the easy part no matter how daunting this first step may feel to some. Developing, growing and retaining the relationship is much more difficult. Let's look at each in turn.

Making contact: There are several ways to make contact with people. Naturally, this is much better when you are looking internally within your organizsation. You can make contact directly via email. For example, if you want to learn more about your marketing unit, check on your intranet site, pick a person in marketing, send them an email introducing yourself and ask if you can schedule some time in their diary for them to talk to you about the team. In most cases the person will agree. You can also take advantage of work events that bring people from different units together and make a point to meet at least five people you don't know.

For external contacts you can start with who you know. You can ask someone you know already to introduce you to someone in their organisation in the department that you are interested in learning more about. This can be facilitated via social networking sites like LinkedIn. Alternatively you can attend networking events that are arranged specifically to bring people from different organisations together.

To help with meeting contacts, especially in the external environment, it is important to always be prepared. It is always annoying when you bump into someone on the subway, during rush hour, and you literally only have a few seconds to say hi before you both have to run off to catch your respective trains. Wouldn't it be great if you had your business card handy for a quick exchange? If you want to build your network, always have a business card handy. It is also good to have an elevator pitch to introduce yourself at networking events or work events that bring people together.

Exercise 11

Try to expand your network this month. You can start internally or go externally if you wish. If you are looking internally, make a list of five people you know but haven't met and make contact. You should look for ways to continually expand your network so repeat this exercise again in a few months' time.

Be bold and also look externally and target to meet five new contacts from different organisations over the coming weeks. Use the suggestions above.

Make a commitment to yourself to take some actions and note your next step to move things forward.

Building a relationship: After the first meeting it's important to follow up soon, either with an email or phone call. Also good to arrange a coffee or lunch as soon as it's convenient so you can get the opportunity to learn more about the other person and vice versa. This applies internally also.

Interestingly, most people won't follow up after that first meeting and within a few months will struggle to remember who that person is. Be proactive when you meet people and find time to get in touch. It is also important when you meet people to make brief notes on the back of their business card about the person. Something that helps you remember the person and may come in useful the next time you meet to kick-start the conversation. For example, you may meet someone who talked about the fact that they had just started a new role. When you catch up with them for coffee weeks later you can kick off the conversation by asking how they are settling into the new role. This is a good way to build rapport very quickly with the other person.

Maintaining a relationship: Building a network doesn't stop after the first follow up. If you don't make contact after that, the relationship will gradually fizzle out. So how do you keep it alive? Well firstly, if you decide this is a relationship you want to keep, make it a point to check in on this person at least once every three months. You can do this via email, text or phone call. Depending on the type of relationship you have, you may choose to meet for coffee or lunch. Ideally you should meet face to face at least once every year.

Managing your network: This is where you can start to distinguish yourself from the pack. Managing your network involves you spending time looking at the makeup of who is in your network and the strength of those relationships. They say your net worth is usually an average of the net worth of those in your active network. This is just a generalisation of course but the statement does have some merit. If you actively network with people who are mostly very senior in the organisational hierarchy you will gradually navigate to the top. The same is the case for the reverse. But it isn't simply about getting to know only those who are of a higher status. It is about networking with people who can contribute to your development the same way you should be contributing to others.

It is good practice to take some time to review who is in your network. Who are you engaging with regularly? Do you have contacts for the various areas in your business life that you don't know anyone outside of your organisation you can call on for advice? If the answer is yes, you have a potential gap in your network so do something about it. If you didn't complete Exercise 11, I recommend that you do.

Exercise 12

Go through your list of contacts, can you remember the last time you met or had a discussion? Are you up to date with where they all are in their careers? Are you up to date with their current location?

Luckily, with social media sites like LinkedIn, finding information of this nature is only a few clicks away.

Make a note of some of your contacts that you need to follow up with and set aside some time in your diary to do so. You can start by sending them an email requesting a catch up.

You also need to consider what is going on with your own life. It is natural that someone in finance will build a network filled with lots of finance people over the years. What happens when this person changes career and moves into the medical industry? They will need to build a whole new set of contacts.

While I have been focusing on calling out the benefits of networking and how to get better at it, I can imagine some people will find a lot of it uncomfortable. Some will even go as far as perceiving some of the above strategies as manipulative, like inviting someone to lunch purely for your own benefit. Let me help put this line of thought to rest. Networking is a win-win game. People make contact with you for the same reason you make contact with them or others: they want something. It's the reason networking events are a success.

If you want to do well in your career and in business you need to master the art of networking. The wider the circle of contacts you engage with, the wider the market for you to explore when you seek out opportunities to advance your career. Networking successfully is a skill that can be learned and perfected over time. As mentioned earlier, it isn't simply about meeting lots of people; you have to also follow up and proactively manage the contacts you have. This requires effort and time to plan and also requires discipline to follow through consistently with your planning. In the next chapter we will focus on execution. Execution is the central philosophy of this book so hopefully you have been carrying out the exercises rather than skipping past them.

#10
Execute like a true professional

In the preceding chapters we have gone through specific concepts and what you need to do to improve your career progression. In each chapter I have defined the concept, explained its relevance and given some guidance on specific actions you need to take. In this final chapter I will focus on what you need to do to be able to make sure you can carry out these actions correctly and consistently, day after day, week after week, month after month and so on.

I will expand on the subject of self-discipline which I mentioned briefly in the introduction. Without self-discipline you will not take the necessary actions when you need to, neither will you carry them out consistently and for long enough to really make a difference.

Planning ahead

One of the most valuable habits you can adopt in your career is the habit of planning your workload in advance. This means taking time in advance to decide how your day will be spent, not just turning up for work and going with the flow. You will be surprised how many people turn up for work and switch on their computers to find out what meetings are in their diaries that they need to attend for the day. They will then decide what to do in the gaps between meetings when they arrive at that free slot. Some will use that time to go through their to-do list and pick an item to work on; others will simply respond to emails until the next meeting. If you do the same, you need to stop this habit immediately as I have disturbing news for you: you are not in control. If you are not already, you will soon find yourself falling behind on some very important tasks and you will not be delivering results at the level that you are capable of if you have to rush through these tasks when they become urgent. More on this later but firstly, let me walk you through an alternative way to manage your workload.

Step 1 – Pick a day in the week when you can dedicate an hour to planning your workload for the following week. I would suggest Friday mornings or sometime during the weekend. Some people prefer to do it first thing Monday morning but I would advise against this as I think Monday being part of that week should also be planned in advance, so Friday or Saturday would be better. This way, you will be able to go straight into action when you turn up for work on Monday.

Step 2 – On a blank sheet of paper, draw out four columns with the following headings: task description, time to complete (minutes), output required and due date. Now list all the important items that need to be done that week and rank them in order of priority. I cover prioritization in the next section. For now, let's stick to whatever approach you use. Finally, note the time required to complete each task. This only needs to be a rough estimate so don't spend too much time trying to be precise. Now describe the output required from this task. This is very important because one of the most common reasons for putting off an important task is not having a clear idea in your mind of the output that is required. Next is to note when the task needs to be completed. Here are two examples in Figure 1 below.

Task description	Time to complete	Output required	Due Date
Prepare slides for Bob on next year's plan	60 mins	3-5 slides showing plans, assumptions, risks and financial impact	27th June
Respond to email from Procurement lead	15 mins	Email showing list of all suppliers to be considered for new bid	Monday at noon, latest

Figure 1 – Weekly workload planning template

Step 3 – Go through your diary for that week and as you go through the meetings you have either accepted to attend or created yourself, check which ones correlate with the items you have noted down as priorities for that week. For example, you have a task to complete on next year's plans for Bob: will any of the meetings you have scheduled help in getting you the required information to complete this task? As you go through each meeting, ask yourself if your attendance is necessary. Is this a meeting that can be pushed back to the following week if not urgent? Are there meetings that are now obsolete because of something else that happened since it got created? People tend to find things to discuss in a meeting whether they are important or not.

Also look at how much time you have allocated to meetings. Is an hour necessary or will 30 minutes be sufficient? Or even 15 minutes. In my experience, some meetings scheduled for an hour will reach an equally effective close if scheduled for 30 minutes instead. People will naturally talk up to the allocated time if the meeting isn't run in a strict and efficient manner.

The objective of this step is to create time for productive work, so once you finish reviewing and altering your diary, highlight all the available time you have and note the number of hours you have each week. The other thing to do while you go through each meeting is to ask yourself what you need to prepare in advance for the meetings that will remain in your diary. Add these to your task list and complete each section accordingly. Re-rank your tasks in order of priority now that you have added new items.

Step 4 – Starting with your top priority, begin creating appointments in your calendar to allocate time to complete each task. For a 15-minute task, create a 15-minute diary entry, for a one-hour task, create a diary entry for an hour, and so on. Be sure to take into account time for logistics. For example, do not schedule an hour to complete a task directly after a meeting in a different building if it will take you 10 minutes to get back to your office. Better to put a 15 minute gap to allow for this so you have an extra five minutes to settle down before you move on to the next task.

I also find it very useful to insert all the necessary information I need in the calendar entry. Take example two in Step 2 as an example: you can copy and paste all the files you need to complete this task into the calendar entry. This is important so when you come to that timeslot you can go straight into action. It's like getting your running gear laid out in the hallway the night before a morning run. This significantly increases the likelihood of you going running than if you didn't do this.

Prioritizing your work

Everything we do at work during a typical work day will fall broadly under one of the following categories: urgent and important, important but not urgent, urgent but not important, not urgent and not important. Let's walk through these in priority order.

Urgent and important

Anything on your task list that is urgent and important is naturally a priority number one item! There is no question here. If you have any of these items on your list, they have to take priority over everything else. Schedule them into your calendar and get them done as quickly as possible. Failing to complete an urgent and important task by its due date will be noticed immediately by your manager and could even get him in trouble with his superiors. Do this once and it will put a negative mark against your name. Do this repeatedly and you will be heading for the exit pretty soon.

What happens if you find yourself with too many urgent and important items? Be proactive about it. Don't hope that you can finish them all and fail to. It is much better to go to your manager in advance and inform him or her of your predicament and let them help you. They may give you some slack on some of the items to help you re-prioritize what needs to be tackled immediately. Avoid doing anything else until you have completed all outstanding urgent and important tasks.

Important but not urgent

This is an area where true professionals distinguish themselves from amateurs. For the amateurs, things that are important but not urgent are ignored and only worked on when they become urgent. True professionals understand that working on important things before they become urgent reduces the number of priority one items on their task list. This gives you two significant benefits.

Firstly, an environment with lots of urgent and important tasks is a stressful one. Your likelihood of failure is enhanced if you constantly find yourself in this position.

Doctors and those in similar emergency professions are obvious exceptions to this rule. For these professions, dealing with urgent and important scenarios is the norm. For the rest of us, this doesn't have to be the case. Working on important but not urgent tasks gives us an opportunity to address important issues before they become urgent and we are able to do this in a much less stressful environment.

An example of an important but not urgent task is the time you put into looking at ways to improve processes within your unit.

Secondly, the quality of your output can be compromised if you have to rush through it to meet a tight deadline. I know some people claim to do their best work under pressure and this may be true, but I believe it's much better to have sufficient time to devote to any given task. This means, for example, if you have to complete a report you will have sufficient time to read through it a second time and correct any errors before submitting it as opposed to having to send in your first draft because you ran out of time.

Once you get some breathing space after completing your urgent and important tasks, this is the next place to dive into. The more you work on important but not urgent tasks, the more in control you will become.

Urgent but not important

Things that are urgent but not important is where the majority of people spend their time, sometimes by convincing themselves that because something is urgent it has to be important. The reality is that people spend their time here to avoid having to work on important items that are not urgent. Even worse, the urgency of these items is also questionable. For example, emails. It doesn't matter how important a task we happen to be working on, when an email comes through we seem to jump on it immediately as though it has to be something extremely important and urgent. Understandably, we can't assess if the email will be important or not so we want to open it quickly to find out, but what do we then do afterward? We either start responding to the mail or we close it and then take a few minutes to start working through our emails while we put the important but not urgent task to one side.

You should never spend time doing urgent but not important tasks while you still have some urgent and important or important but not urgent tasks outstanding. This is a quick way to run into a life of stress and poor, or at best mediocre, performance.

Not urgent and not important

This is the land of social media, reading private emails, calling up friends or colleagues and generally doing all the things you like, most of which are of very little significance or urgency. This is the place most people find themselves when they procrastinate doing those very important tasks.

There is nothing wrong with looking at Facebook, Twitter or LinkedIn, reading private emails or calling up your friends during working hours. It can be a good way to take a break during the day to unwind for a few minutes, but keep it to a minimum. Five minutes at most, then get back into tackling your most important tasks.

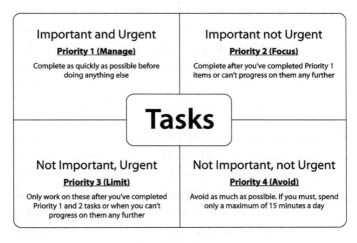

Figure 2 – Prioritisation quadrant

In summary, complete all urgent and important tasks first, then go on to important but not urgent tasks. Ensure you have a good amount of time dedicated to the latter on a weekly basis and you will see a gradual decline in the former. Spend as little time as possible on urgent but not important tasks as soon as you get past the initial urgency, e.g. like taking a call you thought was urgent and finding out it isn't. Tell the person you will ring them back at a later time, preferably after you have completed your higher priority items. Avoid spending time doing things that are not important or urgent. At most, give it a few minutes, then return swiftly to the more important stuff!

Beating procrastination

Procrastination is probably the most common driver for spending time doing things that are not important at the expense of things that are. There will always be one more thing to do before... If you suffer from this, you need to find out the root cause of your procrastination so you can deal with it head on. There are lots of reasons why we procrastinate but I will focus only on my top four.

The task is too big and complex: One of the most common reasons for putting off a task is because it's too big and complex so the thought of doing it becomes too daunting. Whenever the thought of completing this task comes to mind, we find ourselves naturally gravitating to something else, then another, and this continues until we run out of time for the day and that important task remains untouched.

The way to tackle this is to break the task into smaller chunks and pick the natural starting point and go for it without thinking of the other chunks. Finish that chunk first, then pick the next one and you will find that once you get into the swing of it, the task will get much less daunting.

For example, imagine you have been given a task to set up an admin team of 100, in an offshore location. So many questions would spring to mind, especially if you have never done this before:

- Where will they be located?

- How will you conduct the interviews?

- Where will you find candidates?

- What's the budget?

- How will you select the right building?

- What employment laws exist in that country?

   …and the list goes on.

In this situation, it will be easy to find something else that is more urgent to do as it means you can put off facing this very daunting task. **But you don't need to have all the answers before you begin.** A good place to start for something like this could be to sit down with your manager to brainstorm what type of skillset the team needs to have, the preferred salary range, and an ideal start date. So the only thing you need worry about at this stage is booking time in the diary with your manager. After you have had the brainstorm session you can decide what the next best step is and do it. The next action could be to prepare a project plan when you have a clearer idea of what needs to be done, then you can focus on completing each chunk as per your project plan.

What tends to happen in reality is that you will put off doing anything because you are thinking of the answers to all the questions listed above. Eventually you will run out of time and find yourself with a priority one item that has to be completed urgently. Your output on the task will not be your best to say the least.

Lack of motivation: This is when you just can't bring yourself to do the task – either because you don't want to do the task because you don't think you should be doing it, or because it's simply something you know you won't enjoy. Either way, the thought of the task fills you with enough dissatisfaction that you put it off until you have to do it.

A good way to get past this is to ask yourself why the task needs to be completed. What consequences will you or someone else suffer if this task is not completed on time? If there are no consequences then speak to your manager about dumping the task so you can spend your time on something more worthwhile. If there are, then hopefully this realisation will give you the required impetus to act. When you do and you find yourself flagging again, repeat the exercise. Keep doing this until the task is successfully completed.

Fear of failure: This can happen when we are asked to complete a very important task, one where the result could have a significant impact on our overall output for the year. When you get given a task like this, it is easy to become paralysed by the thought of not completing the task to the right standard, and the result is inertia. You become so consumed by the thought that what you produce needs to be perfect and that nothing else will do. Naturally, this can be extremely daunting.

One of the easiest ways to get past this is to just get started. Put the final output out of your mind and promise yourself you will deal with the "polishing" later to make sure it is perfect. For now, you just need to get started. Like the first example, analyse the task and break it down into smaller pieces. Decide on the best piece to tackle first and go for it. Forget about the other pieces for now and focus all of your attention on getting this first piece completed before you pick up the next. You will eventually complete the task, at which point you will have some time to do that final polishing to hopefully get it to the standard that you want. But you won't get to this point if you don't start!

A good example of this is writing a book. If you are concerned about making sure every chapter is perfect, you will never start. If you start and insist on getting each chapter perfect before you get to the next, you will never finish the book. I don't know of anyone who has written a book following this approach. A more successful approach is to complete the first draft of the whole book then go back to the first chapter and work through to the last on a second, more polished draft. Repeat the process until you get to a final draft that you are ready to publish.

Lack of focus: This one can be a real killer of time and is the bedrock of procrastination. You have too many outstanding tasks in your head. You probably have multiple to-do lists: one in your notebook, one on your phone, perhaps even one on another notebook at home, and so on. Your mind is cluttered with half-finished items that whenever you have time to do something, you end up moving from one item to another, sometimes totally confused about what to do next. Whenever you start on something, you find yourself abandoning it after a few minutes to jump on to something else.

If you are in this situation right now you are probably stressed and well behind on a number of deliverables. You will also find that you have been spending a lot of your time on things that are not important because they provide relief when your mind is cluttered. Getting out of this situation will require time and a good dose of self-discipline.

Exercise 13

Block out some time in your diary when you will have at least two hours of uninterrupted time.

Use this time to capture EVERYTHING you have outstanding into ONE list. Yes, ONE list. A good book to read on this is *Getting Things Done* by David Allen.

Once you have captured everything, work through each item and prioritise them using the approach mentioned in the early part of this chapter. Once you have done that, starting with the important and urgent items, schedule when to complete them directly into your calendar and make sure you allocate sufficient time to complete the tasks. When all the important and urgent items are scheduled, move on to the important but not urgent items.

Beating procrastination will help make sure you manage your actions more productively by spending time on tasks that are important and avoid wasting time on tasks that are not.

Conclusion

Before we move on to the final section of this book I suggest you spend some time looking over the 10 rules we have covered to refresh your memory.

1	It's your career
2	Be very clear on why you got hired
3	Respect the performance management process – don't fight it!
4	There are others that matter, besides your line manager
5	Do more than your role requires... and then some
6	Seize opportunities to reinvent yourself
7	Don't do it alone
8	Become an excellent communicator
9	Master the art of networking
10	Execute like a true professional

It's your career so take charge of it and decide what you wish to achieve. Know why you got hired and make sure you're exceeding expectations and this can be monitored via the performance management process.

Get to know your key stakeholders and get them on your side and deliver more than your role requires. Every time you start a new role, see it as a brilliant opportunity to reinvent yourself.

Bring in extra help when you need it and don't try to do things alone. Every very successful person I know had great mentors behind them, so why try to do it alone? The more senior you become, the more critical your communication skills become. Invest time to improve on becoming excellent at getting your message across. Get to know people – lots of people, both within and outside your organisation and keep these relationships alive. It is much easier approaching someone you know for help than someone you don't.

And finally, bring this all together by executing like a pro. Take charge of your time and plan your weeks in advance to make sure you are spending time on the most important activities and staying on top of things. Follow through with your plans because at the end of the day it all comes down to execution. No matter how great your plans are, they won't amount to anything if you don't execute on them.

Your career is a journey not a destination

The essence of this book is to help you make the right decisions and take the right actions during your career. The expected outcome when you implement some of the learnings is that your career journey becomes more rewarding and fulfilling. Notice that I mention career journey not any particular job. Like most people, your career will comprise multiple jobs during your working life, which for most will be between the ages of 20 to about 65, though some people start before age 20 and some go on for much longer than 65.

The typical average in any particular job is about three years. This means the average person will do about 15 different jobs during their working life. It doesn't make much sense therefore if you sacrifice most of your working life pursuing that one big job which could take you a very long time to get, while tolerating or struggling through the first 14 jobs just to land that perfect 15th job to then end your career with.

A better approach is to *enjoy* each role by careful selection taking into consideration your aspirations as well as your strengths. Whenever you find yourself in a situation where you are not enjoying what you are doing, it is time for a correction. First, make sure you understand the root cause of your dissatisfaction. If it is because you are finding the job difficult, have you really applied yourself to it? Put some of the learnings from this book into the job to give yourself a chance to do a great job and see if this improves the situation. Don't be too hasty to ditch the job and move on to something else as you might find the same problems waiting for you. If this happens it's a sign that YOU are the problem, not the job.

If you have really put in the effort and are still struggling to find satisfaction then use **Chapter 1 – It's your career** to help you decide what to do next.

A successful career is not defined by any single moment

Very often I hear people talk about a time when they did something and got promoted and describe it as a career-defining moment. This can sometimes mislead people into believing that to be successful in your career requires you to have those big moments. This isn't entirely accurate. Your career isn't defined by those moments but by the effort you put into all the tasks that you carry out, day by day, week by week, leading up to that moment.

A successful completion of a set of actions leads to the successful completion of a task. Successful completion of lots of tasks leads to the successful completion of an assignment, which leads to success in that particular job. Success in the jobs you do will inevitably lead to a successful career. There is no 'silver bullet' or magic wand, just a simple process of managing each action you take at work, by doing what you need to do when you need to do it and doing it successfully.

Now obviously you won't get things right 100% of the time so mistakes will be made and there are times when you will struggle. When this happens, take the right action to recover. Do some reflection to understand exactly what went wrong then take corrective action, immediately. Don't try to do it alone as this is definitely a time when you need help!

Your career will not be defined by a single failure as failing is necessary for learning as long as you learn from it. This may sound contradictory to the point made above about completing each task successfully, but it isn't. The fact is, whether you like it or not, you will screw up on some tasks and when you do, don't get hung up by it, learn from it and move on. No one goes through life and gets everything right.

Put things into perspective

Working on your career while working in it can be very challenging but you have to do it to be successful. This can sometimes get you so busy doing "stuff" that you forget the big picture. To ensure you maintain focus on the big picture requires you to take some time out regularly to consider what it is you are doing with your life. Now it doesn't matter whether you are successful or not in your career right now, that isn't the point of discussion here. The question here is: are you fulfilled? How often do you come home with a feeling of content, knowing that you have done something that day to make you feel proud? Are you making a positive difference in the environment that you operate in? If your answer to this question is yes, it means you have done something that has made your colleagues, your manager or your customers' lives better. It means you have done something that has made your community better. If you have done this, it means the world is a better place as a result of you being here and this is definitely something you should be proud of!

In the push for promotion and career advancement, it is very easy to forget why you are doing this in the first place. You spend so much time at work trying to build a career that can provide a better life for yourself and your family that you forget to spend time with those that truly matter in your life. Is the relationship with your family worth destroying for the sake of a successful career? I hear some people say they chose family over career but secretly regret not pursuing their dreams. The truth is you don't have to sacrifice one for the other. You can have both as long as you are willing to put in the effort to make this possible. Below are some of the things you should not forget to do while building a successful career.

Spend time with family and friends – If you find yourself, like most of us, working long days during the week, put your work aside at weekends and devote at least one full day 100% to spending time with your family. When you do, be *present* with them so put the smartphone away. There is no point checking your emails while out in a park with your children as you won't be able to disconnect from work and you certainly won't be enjoying the time with your kids either. A good rule of thumb here is to spend time working when you're working and spend time playing when you're playing.

Get proper sleep – This can sometimes seem impossible and there definitely will be periods when it literally is! Make it a point to get to bed by 10 p.m. as often as possible to give yourself a better chance of getting more sleep since you are likely to need to be up early in the morning. Most professionals I know, myself included, need to be up between 5am and 6am so going to bed after 10pm will dramatically reduce the time you will have available for sleeping. In spite of what you might be telling yourself, your body needs up to eight hours sleep per night to recover properly from the stress of the day. There are numerous studies on the negative impact sleep deprivation has on your brain. Whenever you go through continuous periods of less than optimum sleep, maybe due to a tight deadline at work, find an hour and treat yourself to a full body deep tissue massage. An hour of this can have a similar impact on your body of a few hours of deep sleep, so well worth it for the one hour investment of your time and money. In addition, try to adjust your schedule soon afterward to catch up on the lost sleep.

Exercise regularly – I personally find this to be one of the most stress-relieving activities for me. A Saturday morning run after a stressful week at work will do you a lot of good. Ideally, you should aim to exercise for at least 30 minutes three times a week. Find a time that works for you and build it into your routine. If you don't currently exercise regularly, start with doing something twice a week and build up from there. Be disciplined about it, so no excuses when the weather is cold and nasty. Put on the appropriate gear and go for it! When in the office, move regularly and try not to sit at your desk for long periods at a time. Walk across the office and ask someone a question if possible rather than use email or the telephone. Use the stairs sometimes rather than using the lift all the time. The idea here is to be as mobile as you can throughout the day. I sometimes go for a walk when I'm on a conference call that doesn't require me reviewing documents on my screen during the call. This helps me break the time I spend sitting down at my desk and I also find the walk outside very refreshing, which can make the call much more productive.

Engage in recreational activities – If you can't remember the last time you really laughed, I mean to a point of tears coming out of your eyes, then you're not living! Do something fun and occasionally something silly! Take a break from your routine and do something with some friends and family. Try to do something you have never done before from time to time. This mental and physical break from work will energise and invigorate you when you get back to work. There is so much you can do and it doesn't even have to cost a thing. It's amazing how much fun you can have when you wander into a park with a ball and a few friends for an impromptu game of football.

Be mindful of what you eat and when – "You are what you eat" some people say and there is some truth in this. Eating right can have a material impact on your temperament and, naturally, your performance. A protein breakfast is the best way to start the day. Skipping breakfast is not – plain and simple. There are so many options available to make this possible for even the most time-constrained of us so there are really no excuses here. Eat fruit during the day to stay energised and avoid reaching for those sugary items that only provide a short-term boost. Having a banana late in the afternoon will do much more good than a bar of chocolate.

Give back to others – Look for others to mentor as you look for a mentor for yourself. I have found mentoring to be a very rewarding endeavour and have been actively mentoring others for over 10 years. You'll be amazed at what you can offer to someone else with very little experience. If you have a mentoring scheme at work, make yourself available to take on mentees and devote some of your time to helping them climb up the career ladder. I can't exaggerate how important this is and how worthwhile it will be to you.

Exercise 14

If you don't currently mentor anyone, spend a few minutes and put together a quick plan to find three mentees within the next four weeks.

As mentioned above, if you have a mentoring scheme at work, join it and volunteer to be a mentor. In addition, speak with people you know and ask them to refer suitable candidates to you who are interested in finding a mentor.

If you already mentor, can you take on more? If so, follow the approach above.

Make a commitment today to take action and plan it accordingly.

Most of what you have read in this book requires effort. Effort to think, effort to plan, effort to act. What will have the biggest impact is that you act. Very often we find that most people are great at coming up with ideas and knowing what to do. Some go ahead and plan what to do, but very few go as far as taking the necessary action to bring that plan to fruition. Even fewer will do this consistently for as long as is necessary to guarantee long-term success.

Don't spend too much time deliberating on things. Life is passing you by while you are still thinking. What you are planning today to do tomorrow someone thought of yesterday and is doing today. Opportunities don't sit there until whenever you are ready. Someone else takes them! Think fast and analyse quickly, then act decisively and make a difference.

Take a jump and see where you land... I wish you the very best in your career journey.

About the author

BUCHI ONWUGBONU has more than 10 years' experience in leadership roles for large corporates, SMEs and public services organisations. He has had senior roles in finance, consulting, operations and commercial, globally, working in companies like British Airways, Technicolor and Accenture. He is currently a Managing Director in the Telecoms and Technology sector.

Buchi has a passion for helping people develop their careers and actively mentors aspiring leaders around the globe. He maintains the fundamental belief that you can take your career anywhere you want as long as you're willing to put in the work. He has demonstrated this by successfully changing career paths on numerous occasions. From finance into consulting, then into operations, and more recently taking on a role as Managing Director to run a portfolio of standalone businesses.

Buchi loves running at the weekends to unwind and also traveling around the world with his family. He lives in the UK with his wife and two daughters.

Notes:

Notes:

Notes:

Notes: